# New News Out of Africa

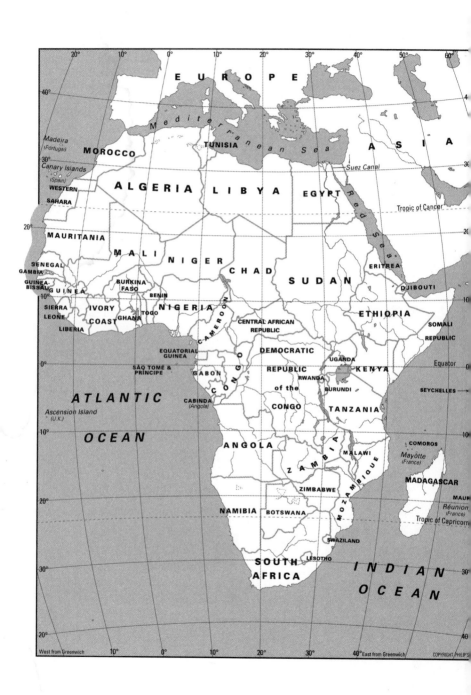

# New News Out of Africa

## Uncovering Africa's Renaissance

*Charlayne Hunter-Gault*

**OXFORD**
UNIVERSITY PRESS
2006

# OXFORD
UNIVERSITY PRESS

Oxford University Press, Inc., publishes works that further
Oxford University's objective of excellence
in research, scholarship, and education.

Oxford    New York
Auckland    Cape Town    Dar es Salaam    Hong Kong    Karachi
Kuala Lumpur    Madrid    Melbourne    Mexico City    Nairobi
New Delhi    Shanghai    Taipei    Toronto

With offices in
Argentina    Austria    Brazil    Chile    Czech Republic    France    Greece
Guatemala    Hungary    Italy    Japan    Poland    Portugal    Singapore
South Korea    Switzerland    Thailand    Turkey    Ukraine    Vietnam

Published by Oxford University Press, Inc.
198 Madison Avenue, New York, NY 10016
www.oup.com

Library of Congress Cataloging-in-Publication Data
Hunter-Gault, Charlayne.
New news out of Africa / Charlayne Hunter-Gault.
p. cm.
Includes bibliographical references and index.
ISBN-13: 978-0-19-517747-3
ISBN-10: 0-19-517747-9
1. Africa, Sub-Saharan—Politics and government—1960- .
2. Africa, Sub-Saharan—Press coverage.    I. Title.
DT352.8.H86 2006
968'.0009'049—dc22
2005023124

Frontispiece map: Copyright © 2005 Philip's, adapted from Philip's Children's Atlas

1 3 5 7 9 8 6 4 2

Printed in the United States of America
on acid-free paper

# Contents

# Acknowledgments

*I*f I acknowledged all the people who helped make this book possible, the pages would exceed the length of the book. So let me paint with broad brush strokes and thank the African family, both on the continent and in the diaspora, who helped me to see the things I had not yet learned to see and to trust what I was seeing through the prism of experiences that made me who I am. But I would also like to single out members of the family who made an extra-special contribution. First and foremost is Henry Louis "Skip" Gates Jr., who listened well and heard my frustrations about the lack of coverage of Africa in America. As a result, I was honored to accept his invitation to become the 2003 McMillan-Stewart Fellow at the W. E. B. Du Bois Institute for Afro-American Research at Harvard University, delivering three lectures in February 2003 that became this book. I am grateful for his infectious enthusiasm, for his ongoing encouragement, and for the warm hospitality shown me by him and his colleagues at the Institute and throughout the university.

I am also indebted to Shadrack Gutto, head of the Pretoria-based Centre for African Renaissance Studies, to John Stremlau, former professor of international affairs and former head of the Department of International Relations at the University of the Witwatersrand in Johannesburg, and to Dr. Helen Rees, director of the Reproductive Health Research Unit of the Department of Obstetrics and Gynaecology at the University of the Witwatersrand, whose dedicated work in AIDS prevention is significantly advancing the fight against HIV and AIDS, especially as it affects women and girls. Their critical wisdom gave me the inspiration I needed to get the job done. Additionally, there are the friends and colleagues who are always there for me and in this instance came to my rescue in a variety of special ways: Xoli Moloi, Allana Finley, and Yollette Yohaar.

Then there are my husband, Ronald, my daughter, Suesan, and my son, Chuma, who just do what they need to do to help me be who I am—sometimes a challenge! And always, remembering my late mother, Althea, my enduring inspiration.

Finally, I want to thank Elda Rotor, a gentle genius of an editor, whose patience with me will surely serve her well in the other profession she came to as she helped me give birth to this book. Luka is a lucky boy!

Charlayne Hunter-Gault
Johannesburg, South Africa
June 29, 2005

# Introduction

*I* once had a journalism professor who used to ask on the first day of class: "What are the news?" To which he would hasten to provide this answer to his befuddled students: "Not a single new."

I never quite got the point, but I still remember the exercise of forty-something years ago, especially when I am confronted with "not a single new" in the general coverage of Africa.

On my annual trips home to the United States from South Africa, I am constantly amazed at how little of the good news—or what I prefer to call the "new news"—about Africa is getting through to most Americans. With rare exceptions, the people I encounter, from all walks and stations in life, still think of Africa as the "dark continent," made darker still by the ravages of AIDS and the ongoing conflicts that occasionally produce enough carnage to merit a minute or two on a television newscast. But just as not all Africans are dark-skinned, neither is the continent a dark place. In fact, the continent of Africa is a multifarious place, comprising fifty-four countries, home to some 800 million people, encompassing a multitude of ethnicities and races and a complex range of eccentricities. At the moment, it is a continent at a critical moment in its history, with its nations undergoing

change, albeit at different stages, and in many cases transformation. What follows is a modest attempt to capture this moment
of a continent in motion—from the vast and dramatic changes
aimed at correcting the historical wrongs of apartheid South
Africa at the continent's southernmost tip to those taking place
above and around South Africa and to the east and west of it. It
is an attempt not to give a definitive account but to use a few
examples from my experiences and observations over the past
eight years to create a status report of a continent in a hopeful
transition, albeit one that is often slow and sometimes madden-
ingly regressive. I will leave it to the Africanist scholars, analysts,
and pundits to do the definitive studies—or perhaps myself,
further on in my "journey to the horizons." Rather, this little
book is an attempt to share the motivations that led me to Africa
and to illuminate some of the examples that speak to what I call
"new news" out of Africa.

New News Out of Africa

# chapter One

# South Africa, Then and Now

Sometime after I had learned to read, I came across a poem that spoke to me directly. It was Countee Cullen's "Heritage":

> What is Africa to me:
> Copper sun or scarlet sea,
> Jungle star or jungle track,
> Strong bronzed men, or regal black
> Women from whose loins I sprang
> when the birds of Eden sang?[1]

It wasn't until I reached adulthood and entered the professional world that I finally set foot on African soil. But even in my earliest childhood, before I dreamed of being a journalist, there was an Africa in my life, though it was only on the silver screen, and depicted in ways that, in retrospect, make me sad: stereotypes of Africans as hapless or even demonic. And though such images were a part of the Saturdays I spent at "the show"—the segregated movie theater in the small southern town of Covington, Georgia, where I grew up—I was an only child whose salvation from that unique loneliness was refuge in the imagination. And so I was able to make leaps in my mind over the strong, muscular image of the heroic white Tarzan and his beloved Jane swinging through the trees of the jungle, saving deserving African natives while savaging the rest. I cannot remember any of the plots, only that the hero was always white. Away from the jungle of the silver screen, I happily created my own African jungle in the enchanting wooded area behind my house.

Years later I went on holiday with my family in South Africa's Eastern Cape, drawn in part by Noel Mostert's description of it as a place where "blue gray mountains fold across one another, and tumble down to surf strewn boulder or accompany long white beaches. . . . No where else on earth do sea and sky and walled granite and shining sand, convey any impression of nature more placidly reposeful, more grandly and anciently benign. Calmly surfeited by its own overwhelmingly incremental fortune of light and colour, ceaselessly spent all around on sea, sand and forested slopes, it impresses one as being a natural world serenely dispassionate about itself, without connivance or hidden design."[2]

I found all that, and more, when I was hiking one day with my grown children, Suesan and Chuma, and my husband, Ronald, through Tsitsikamma National Park, along a trail edged by brush so thick it shut out the bright sunlight dancing on the water near the secluded, pristine beach to which we were headed. Suddenly I began to shriek: "It's here! It's here!"

My children and husband froze in their tracks, thinking I had encountered a puff adder or a black mamba. But in fact what I had just realized was that one of my dreams had come true. For years I had cherished and nurtured the memory of the jungle I had fantasized about in my backyard in Covington as an ideal place where I felt in touch with nature, with myself, and with something lost but not forgotten in primal memory. And now it was real and more wonderful than I had imagined.

"It's my dream!" I continued to my family. "I am actually walking in my dreams from yesterday. I am in a real jungle, in Africa!"

Well, not quite. But about as close to one as ever-encroaching modern civilization allows.

So . . .

what is Africa to me?
Copper sun or scarlet sea,
Jungle star or jungle track . . .

Yes, it is all that to me, and more than even the poet who penned those lines ever could have experienced or imagined.

In this book I explore what Africa is to me in the context of a transforming South Africa—a country that is substantially different from what it was during its violent and tumultuous last decade of apartheid, when it assaulted my emotions and challenged my professional distance on my first trip there. I will also examine some of the struggles of sub-Saharan nations as they seek to find their place among the global family of democratic nations—the most hopeful development since the end of colonialism. And finally, I look at how South Africa and Africa are portrayed to the world, both by those of us in the foreign media and by those who claim it as their own.

I wish to declare up front that I am confronted by a peculiar challenge: seeing the continent and the people who inhabit it through the prism of growing up black and female in America during a time of transition, if not transformation, in this country. I was born at a time when the United States still embraced the part of itself that denied people of color the same place in its world as whites. During my young adulthood we were waging a moral struggle for our rights in America, insisting that we be allowed to embrace our destiny without the racist obstruction that had stood in the way of our fathers and mothers, grand-fathers and grandmothers. At the same time, sub-Saharan Africa was throwing off the yoke of colonialism. It was during these years that Africa to me became more than "Copper sun or scar-let sea, / Jungle star or jungle track."

President John F. Kennedy's brother, Robert F. Kennedy, then attorney general of the United States, articulated the con-nection at a critical time in my own history, as well as America's and Africa's. RFK had come to speak at the University of Georgia just after a high school classmate, Hamilton Holmes, and I had walked through the wall of white resistance and became the first two black students to enroll there in the univer-sity's 176-year history. While we had broken down the legal barrier of the color bar, the white racist mentality was still alive and well, still threatening. But in the context of the United States' Cold War contest with the Soviet Union for global domi-nance, the Kennedys needed a transformed American South. As the Africanist scholar Salih Booker put it: "With decolonization in Africa, apartheid in America became an untenable liability for Washington in its battle with Moscow for global influence. It was an era of intensified struggle and of high hopes for both Africans and their lost relations in the US."[3]

As I sat in a sea of mostly white faces, Robert Kennedy began to speak to a crowd as hostile to him as it was to me. This is how I remembered it in my book *In My Place*:

Kennedy talked about the challenge of international Communism—the defining context of the Cold War era in which we were living—and about organized crime. And then he entered the real danger zone—civil rights, which Southerners unabashedly viewed as a "communist con-spiracy." He started out by saying that "Southerners have a respect for candor and plain talk. They certainly don't like hypocrisy," and he proceeded to lay some candor on them.

He pointed out that "50 percent of the countries in the United Nations are not white; that around the world, in Africa, South America, and Asia, people whose skins are a different color from ours are on the move to gain their measure of freedom and liberty. . . . From the Congo to Cuba, from South Vietnam to Algiers, in India, Brazil, and Iran, men and women and children are straightening their backs and listening—to the evil promises of Communist tyranny and the honorable promises of Anglo-American liberty. And those people will decide not only their future but how the cause of freedom fares in the world. . . ."

I was thinking to myself at this moment, This is a helluva speech, and wondering how much he had been told about the University of Georgia "situation," if, indeed, he even knew our names. I vaguely heard, "In the worldwide struggle, the graduation at this university . . ." and then I heard words that almost knocked me off my seat: ". . . of Charlayne Hunter and Hamilton Holmes will without question aid and assist the fight against Communism, political infiltration, and guerrilla warfare."

From this point on, I sat there in a mild state of shock. . . . Did I hear him right? Did he really say that our graduation was going to assist in the defeat of Communism? guerrilla warfare? And what was that other thing?[4]

At the end of the day, Hamilton Holmes and I, along with thousands of America's black children and adults, had our victory over racism and bigotry: the two of us graduated in May 1963, thanks to the Supreme Court's 1954 decision in *Brown v. Board of Education*, which caused "separate but equal" to disappear from the lexicon of American discourse (though, alas, it did not lead to the eradication of racial inequalities in education, which continue).

While America made (or was forced to make) the right choices in that battle, the country went on to make a series of wrong choices in several newly liberated nations of Africa, backing despots—such as Congo's Mobutu Sese Seko—who abused their people, denying them the promise of freedom held out by independence. The imperatives of the Cold War led Republicans and Democrats alike to make choices inimical to African progress as the United States buttressed regimes it deemed necessary to protect against an "arc of crisis from Asia to South Africa" resulting from Soviet expansionism.[5]

Thus Nelson Mandela and his African National Congress (ANC), waging armed struggle against the apartheid government in South Africa from inside and outside the country, were seen by some in the West, including the United States, as terrorists rather than liberators. The United States aligned itself with the apartheid regime and with movements the all-white regime supported, such as Jonas Savimbi's UNITA in Angola, leading to a decades-long civil war that killed or injured millions of Angolans and ended only with Savimbi's death in February 2002.

During this period African Americans such as myself more often than not sided with the liberation movements, despite our own commitment to nonviolence during our struggle for liberation from American-style apartheid. (Even South Africa's Archbishop Desmond Tutu, a proponent of nonviolence and winner of the 1984 Nobel Peace Prize, defended the concept of the "just war.")

As an African American in journalism, a profession that requires detachment, I have experienced the "double consciousness" phenomenon captured by the activist historian W. E. B.

Du Bois: "One ever feels his two-ness,—an American, a Negro; two souls, two thoughts, two unrecognized strivings; two warring ideals in one dark body, whose dogged strength alone keeps it from being torn asunder."[6] Of course, Du Bois was writing of the conflicts African Americans experienced living in America. But I often find myself thinking about this description as I am challenged to reconcile my spiritual, cultural, and historical connections to Africa not only with the detachment my profession requires but also with the way I am perceived in Africa: as a foreigner, as an American, and sometimes even as white!

Today I live in South Africa, and often meet friends—black and white, young and not so young—for drinks, a meal, or a bit of shopping at Rosebank, an increasingly upscale shopping center in Johannesburg's northern suburbs. It is 2006, several years into South Africa's postapartheid democracy, and we are all totally unselfconscious about being there. But I cannot go to Rosebank without recalling that it was my first point of entry into a very different Johannesburg two decades ago. In 1985, when I arrived to cover the struggle against the apartheid regime, South Africa filled the old news bill, with its bubbling brew of conflict and chaos and one-dimensional characters (black victims and white oppressors), and the world's media were all over the story.

I had just flown into South Africa with a team of four Americans, joining three South Africans and a British producer. We arrived as the world's image of South Africa was being formed by what viewers saw on their television screens—relentless violence by state security forces against mostly defenseless black men, women, and children who had but a single, simple wish: to be treated as human beings, the equal of other human beings. And for that, they were being subjected to some of the worst, most brutal violence the world had ever known. We had come to

South Africa for the *MacNeil/Lehrer NewsHour* to try to penetrate the cliché that apartheid had become—a nearly indecipherable mass of brutalizer and brutalized, victimizer and victim, evil versus good. Aside from the jailed Mandela, virtually none of those embroiled in this conflict were known by name, especially outside South Africa.

By the time the other Americans, my British producer, and I arrived, the South African government had come to see journalists as the enemy, too. The apartheid regime had declared a state of emergency, giving it broad powers to restrict any and all movement, especially in and around the sprawling, poor black townships—densely populated black enclaves with hundreds of matchbox houses, most without electricity or running water, where all too often children had to play amid slimy, fetid streams of garbage and human waste. These "locations," as they were also called by the white authorities, miles outside the white cities, had been engineered by the apartheid state for easy containment in case of trouble.

My team had had to secure permission to enter the country, detailing our professions and why we were there. So the state security agents knew not only that we were there but also where we were. This is where Rosebank came in.

We were staying in a moderately priced small hotel in Rosebank, chosen because it would be easy for us to lug our television gear in and out of our rooms. Most journalists stayed at the more popular Carleton downtown, but as a high-rise, it was not as user-friendly for television crews. So the Rosebank Hotel became our home for the next two months, and while there were few other journalists staying there with us, the state security forces were always (and not so subtly) present, ever watchful.

Early in our stay we made a forbidden foray into the township of Kwa-Thema, about forty-five minutes outside of Johannesburg, where we were confronted with ugly reality sooner than I was emotionally prepared for. Sister Agatha, a sympathetic nun, had taken us to see for ourselves the kind of senseless, unprovoked violence the state was unleashing day in and day out on the people of the township. We walked to a house where we were greeted by a tall, heavy-set woman who moved with a lumbering gait and had difficulty lowering herself into the chair in her tiny living room, where we had gone to hear her story. Assured by Sister Agatha that it was all right to talk freely, the woman, whom we would call Teresa in our broadcast, began to tell the story of how black police agents had come to her place of business, an unlicensed bar known as a shebeen (prevalent all over the townships as the only places black people could go to socialize), and after a few drinks began taunting and eventually beating her, finally taking her to the police station. She said they never told her why, although they may have thought she was connected somehow with the antiapartheid activists who were slowly but surely making the country ungovernable. She insisted she was not.

As she told us her story, she showed us her scars—her huge breasts blue and green from the bruises sustained during the beating, her head caked with dried blood from the many blows, her back bearing the scars of the sjambok, the long black rubber whip favored by the police in their confrontations with activists. Even though I'd grown up in the American South, where I'd heard of lynchings and other brutalities of segregation, I'd never seen the victims in the flesh. Now I was up close and personal with the raw sight of hatred's work, and it made its way into my soul like a slow-burning fuse. Halfway through her story, I excused myself to go outside and get hold of my emotions. I only made it as far as the kitchen, where I collapsed on the floor, unable to hold back the rush of tears.

Sister Agatha suspected something was wrong and followed me into the kitchen. But when she and a neighbor of the victim began comforting me, I felt ashamed and embarrassed at my lack of control—I wasn't the one who should be comforted. That jolted me back to reality and allowed me to collect myself enough to go back in and record the rest of Teresa's story. We left, promising to return the following day to shoot scenes in and around the shebeen. But on the way out, we were apprehended by security agents and given a stern warning to leave and not come back without a permit—impossible to obtain, of course— or face the consequences. We didn't know exactly what those consequences were, but with so much brutality all around, we didn't have to let our imaginations run too far. It was part of the state's disingenuous dance—like pretending to be democratic while denying the country's black majority its civil rights and abusing its human rights. Now its agents were pretending there was, in fact, a process for getting permission to report on the unrest in the townships, when in fact the only thing the process was designed to do was just the opposite: stall and stall until we got too frustrated to go on or the moment had passed. Fortunately, they didn't take our tape.

Back in Johannesburg, our eagerness to proceed blinded us to a certain reality. We gave the tape to a company for transcribing, which is routine in America. But this was not America. After two days, in the early morning, a stocky white man came knocking on our door. I was asleep in one part of the suite, and my white South African colleague, producer Cliff Bestall, was working in the adjoining room, where we had set up our editing equipment. Awakened by the knocking, I lay there listening to the unfolding conversation. The newcomer was saying his machines had broken down and he wouldn't be able to transcribe the tape.

"Ever?" my colleague asked.

"Never," the man replied.

When the door finally closed, my South African colleague gestured to me silently, indicating that I should dress rapidly, grab my pocketbook, put the tape in it, and get the hell out of there. Even if we couldn't get back into the township, we had just barely enough to tell the story. But without that tape, we had no story and no time to find another, particularly if the police prevented us from returning to the township.

Emerging into Tyrwhitt Street, we drove around Rosebank. The area looked stunningly hospitable, with its tree-lined streets, masses of stunning deep pink bougainvillea, tall and cocky orange and purple birds of paradise, and spacious homes —most of which were hidden behind high walls designed to keep out what the white inhabitants thought of as the black hordes clamoring for liberation, if not the family jewels. The exception was "their blacks"—the faithful domestics and "garden boys," many of whom lived on the premises in tiny, cramped cubicles outside the main house, while others made the daily trek from the "locations" in the overloaded, poorly maintained minivans that served as a major form of public transportation for blacks. (Years later they were to be dubbed "mobile coffins" by the country's second black president, Thabo Mbeki, because of the incredibly high death toll due to ill-trained and often unlicensed drivers, poor vehicle maintenance, and near-suffocating levels of overcrowding.) But as welcoming as Rosebank may have seemed to us, for those who depended on these minivans for transport, its splendor stood in stark contrast to the townships in all their squalor.

Within the hour, Cliff decided to take the tape to the BBC, which had been raided the previous week, on the assumption that the state security agents would not be coming there again so soon. So we headed for the modest house they worked from and placed our precious package behind a row of books on one of the dustiest shelves of the bookcase.

By week's end, we had managed to sneak back into Kwa-Thema and complete the story, dodging state security agents all the while. The story of Teresa became part of a prize-winning series called "Apartheid's People," cited for being the first up-close look at all of the people who were South Africa's victims— the oppressors as well as the oppressed.

It would be some time before I began to think in terms of "new news" out of South Africa, but it was during this period that the seeds were sown not only for a new South Africa but also for news that went beyond the simplistic "black versus white" story being transmitted to the outside world. To be sure, it was a case of the white minority oppressing the black majority, but there were many shades of gray, including the whites, coloreds, and Indians fighting above- and underground on the side of the anti-apartheid forces.

When I came back to live in South Africa twelve years later, South Africa had had what many were calling its "miracle."

The oppressed were in, the oppressors (mostly) out. There had been no "eye for an eye" retribution, no civil war, thanks to a process as unique as finding a country still effectively colonized in the latter half of the twentieth century. South Africans had ended their decades-long obscenity of minority rule not on the battlefield but at the negotiating table, and as fractious and often bitter as that process had been, within a short span of time South Africa had become, in the words of Allister Sparks, one of its most insightful chroniclers, "another country"—democratic and nonracial, where Nelson Mandela voted for the first time in his life in 1994, at age seventy-five, just days before becoming the first black president of the country.

The day before Mandela took his first steps as a free man on February 11, 1990, I was spending a quiet Saturday morning in my house on Manhattan's Upper West Side when my *MacNeil/ Lehrer NewsHour* producer, Jackie Farmer, called me, sounding breathless.

"Turn on the TV," she shouted, in a way that left me no choice but to do so without taking time to ask why. Soon I heard South Africa's president, F. W. de Klerk, making the announcement so many had hoped against hope they would hear in their lifetime: Nelson Mandela was about to be a free man, released from his life sentence after serving twenty-seven years in prison. Instantly, in my mind's eye, I conjured an image of Nelson Mandela leaving Victor Vester prison, his wife, Winnie, beaming broadly beside him—and me reporting the story.

My producer read my mind. "When shall I book the flight?" she asked matter-of-factly.

"The first one out to London," I said without hesitation.

In those days, international sanctions on South Africa prevented direct flights to the country. Moreover, the regime had not been generous in granting visas to foreign journalists. But with Nelson Mandela soon to be waving to masses of people who had thought they'd never see this in their lifetime—the tangible embodiment of freedom's promise—at that moment I believed anything was possible.

Before leaving New York, I managed to gain a groundbreaking joint interview with South Africa's ambassador to the United Nations, Steven Buekes, and the African National Congress's UN representative, Tebogo Mafole—the first time they had appeared together publicly. The worm was indeed turning. The interview was taped and edited into a documentary I had been preparing with journalists Danny Schechter and Rory O'Connor, following earlier reports that sometime in the near future a release might be in the offing. The documentary had carried the working title *Waiting for Mandela*, but after the news was announced, the documentary was hastily renamed *Free at Last* and scheduled to run at 9 p.m. Sunday night, the day of his release. The production team went into high gear, working frenziedly throughout the night Saturday to change all references to previous uncertainty about his release, making it appear that we'd had some kind of inside knowledge. By the time the program aired, containing the two interviews I'd done, I was watching it from the lounge at John F. Kennedy International Airport, waiting to board a flight to London.

In London, I briefly met with Thabo Mbeki, then the head of the department of international affairs for the African National Congress. He directed my colleague and me to the South African embassy but didn't accompany us himself. De Klerk had unbanned the ANC on February 2, nine days before releasing Mandela, but individual members had not been indemnified, and Mbeki was still uncertain of the reception an exile associated with Umkhonto we Sizwe, the military wing of his movement, among other things, might get.

We arrived in South Africa on Tuesday and caught a cab at Johannesburg International Airport. In the old days, foreign blacks coming into that airport had to be classified as "honorary whites" in order to be admitted to the country, which caused some blacks to refuse to visit. But there we were, and within no time, the black taxi driver was telling us excitedly that Mandela was scheduled to appear at the big First National Bank Stadium (widely known as FNB) in the black township of Soweto—"the mother city of black urban South Africa," as Mandela has called it. We immediately changed our plans to go to the hotel and asked the driver to take us directly to FNB instead. When we arrived at the huge stadium, we found a festive throng of some 120,000 South Africans of every description, many of them young men raising the dry red dust as they chanted and did the toi-toi—a martial dance of defiance made popular in the days of anti-apartheid uprisings. Most of them had not been born when Mandela was sent to prison. But even from behind bars, he had been their beacon in the stormy seas of apartheid, and now his light was about to shine on them directly.

Lugging our suitcases, we tried without success to get close to the field, but then retreated into the stands, where the only seats left were up in what we in the segregated American South used to call the "crow's nest." We sat there among the wildly exuberant crowd for about an hour before Mandela's entourage arrived, swinging and swaying to the songs that had been the lifeblood of the struggle—the deep, defiant, and throaty voices of these masses now rising victorious toward the blue sky and blazing sun above.

Mandela arrived with Winnie in a helicopter that landed in the middle of the stadium. The crowd went wild but remained orderly. Mandela waved to the assembled throng and walked, a bit unsteadily, to the platform.

"Today, my return to Soweto fills my heart with joy," he told the mostly silent crowds. "At the same time I also return with a deep sense of sadness. Sadness to learn that you are still suffering under an inhuman system. The housing shortage, the schools crisis, unemployment and the crime rate still remain."[7]

But, in what came to be vintage Mandela, he also spoke of the shortcomings of his own supporters. "As proud as I am to be part of the Soweto community, I have been greatly disturbed by the statistics of crime that I read in the newspapers. Although I understand the deprivations our people suffer I must make it clear that the level of crime in the township is unhealthy and must be eliminated as a matter of urgency."[8]

Mandela ended, as he recounted in his autobiography, by "opening my arms to all South Africans of goodwill and good intentions, saying that 'no man or woman who has abandoned apartheid will be excluded from our movement toward a non-racial, united and democratic South Africa based on one-person one-vote on a common voters' roll. . . . It was the dream I cherished when I entered prison at the age of forty-four, but I was no longer a young man, I was seventy-one, and I could not afford to waste any time."[9]

His remarks were brief and so was his visit—the result, I later learned, of fears in the ANC of a possible assassination attempt. Still, however brief his appearance, another chapter in South Africa's history was written that day, and I felt the awesome thrill of being there to witness it.

Jackie and I returned to our hotel, the excitement of the day partially eclipsing our anxieties over how we were going to make good on our promise to Jim Lehrer of getting a Mandela interview. The next day, I dispatched her to the Soweto house of the Mandelas while I worked the phones, calling activists and others I had met when in South Africa five years earlier, some of whom I had kept in contact with. On the ground in Soweto, some twenty minutes beyond the city center, Jackie made all the necessary contacts, reestablishing our bona fides and trying to set us apart from the growing mass of journalists that had begun camping out at the flimsy gate at number 8115 in Orlando West, the tiny four-room matchbox house Mandela had left some twenty-seven years before, and where now a goat stood hitched to a tree in the garden for a later welcoming sacrifice.

Zwelakhe Sisulu, the son of Mandela's fellow ANC member imprisoned at Robben Island, Walter Sisulu, was coordinating the press, and told Jackie that I should come on Friday. It turned out this was the day all media were being given a chance to interview Mandela—ten minutes each for all the major news organizations. Ted Koppel from ABC's *Nightline* and I were the only two to get thirty minutes—I think because of our consistent reporting of the story over time.

I almost lost my breath at my first up-close sighting of Mandela, who was wearing a smartly tailored gray suit, white shirt, and red tie. Though he was smiling, he seemed very formal and reserved. At the first opportunity, I bounded past the relatively lax security and introduced myself. "I'm Charlayne Hunter-Gault and I'll be interviewing you later," I announced with all the confidence and charm I could muster. He smiled, nodded, and politely said, "Er, yes, I am looking forward to it."

Well, that was my opening. Everyone had seen our little exchange, and while no doubt his response to me was due in part to his disarming graciousness, which would become one of his trademarks, that and the fact that I'd established myself with some of his closest advisors enabled me to remain constantly at his side, except for when he sat for what seemed like an endless number of ten-minute interviews underneath a tall, leafy tree in the tiny yard.

When my time finally came, I asked Zwelakhe if perhaps Mandela could take a bit of a break and have a cup of tea so that he would be refreshed for the half-hour interview. I wanted to go beyond what the other journalists were getting in their ten minutes, something more intimate and revealing about what had sustained him for the twenty-seven years behind bars, and how that would affect his attitude, especially toward those who had put him there. I also wanted to get him to talk about his vision for the country. Zwelakhe agreed, but warned me that Mandela was unlikely to speak of his time on Robben Island: "I understand what you are going to try to do, but those old guys have a culture of prison. They talk about it only among themselves. But you can try."

By the time Mandela sat in the chair in front of me, the sun was setting too rapidly for my producer's comfort. But I wasn't going to let that stop me—I would have done the interview even if the heavens had opened up—so I told Jackie to be cool. Then I explained to Mandela at length how my own background in civil rights in America had led by logical extension to my intense interest in the South African struggle.

Mandela listened attentively. At one point, when I paused for air, he asked: "Do you know Miss Maya Angelou?"

"Why, of course," I answered. "She is one of our national treasures."

Mandela smiled. "Yes," he said, "I know her. We used to read her poetry in prison."

What a moment! Of course, that was about as much as he said about prison during that half hour.

Later I came to understand his reticence when I read his auto-biography, *Long Walk to Freedom*. He explained that when he had gone to prison, there were no television cameras and certainly no press conferences.

"From my very first press conference I noticed that journalists were as eager to learn about my personal feelings and relationships as my political thoughts," he wrote. "This was new to me; when I went to prison, a journalist would never have thought of asking questions about one's wife and family, one's emotions, one's most intimate moments. While it was understandable that the press might be interested in these things, I nevertheless found their curiosity difficult to satisfy. I am not and never have been a man who finds it easy to talk about his feelings in public. I was often asked by reporters how it felt to be free, and I did my best to describe the indescribable, and usually failed."[10]

Nevertheless, I had a wonderful interview that opened a small window into the soul of the man and his mission. It was also the beginning of a relationship that frequently permitted me special access, sometimes to the dismay of his often over-protective handlers. I can remember that at the time of his eighty-fifth birthday, in 2003, the media had been invited to the Johannesburg home he shared with his third wife, Graça Machel, the widow of Mozambican freedom fighter and later president Samora Machel. Mandela had married her on his eightieth birthday, and this was their fifth anniversary as well as his birthday. A huge bash was planned for later, to be attended by invited guests and dignitaries from all over the world, including Oprah Winfrey and former president Bill Clinton and his wife, Senator Hillary Rodham Clinton.

On this occasion, a group of young physically and/or mentally challenged children had been invited to share the morning at Mandela's home. After stepping down as president, Mandela had devoted much of his time to children—including his own three surviving children, thirty-nine grandchildren, and six great-grandchildren—along with Graça's two children and her grandchild. But his embrace of children extends far beyond his own. In 1994 he founded the Nelson Mandela Children's Fund, donating a third of his salary as president to getting it started and keeping it going. The fund was initially established to help the needy and impoverished children of South Africa, with Mandela raising millions of dollars at home and abroad. But the scourge of HIV/AIDS has since led the foundation to narrow its focus to AIDS orphans, especially those heading households. Additionally, Mandela has joined his wife, Graça, in working with UNICEF's international appeals for children, lobbying around the world for the right of children "to grow to adulthood in health, peace and dignity."[11]

When Mandela came into the room that day, he spent a lot of time talking with these children, asking them about themselves and telling them they should believe they had no obstacles in their paths to fulfill their dreams. He spoke with the passion of a caring grandfather. Some of the children were able to respond, others not. But it was clear from their expressions that most were thrilled to be in Mandela's presence. One young cancer victim, bald from the chemotherapy and wheelchair-bound, with only a short time to live, told me it was a "dream come true."

Following his greetings to all of them, he and his wife were led to a giant birthday cake just in front of the children. The media, instructed earlier not to ask questions, were off to the side, but within a few feet of the cake and the Mandelas.

After their joint cutting of the cake, Mandela turned in our direction, and I caught his eye.

"How's it feel to be eighty-five?" I shouted from the floor, where I was sitting in front of my cameraperson.

He smiled and said, "It feels wonderful."

As his handlers glared, I dared to take advantage of the fact that his attention was still focused on me, and called out, "And what about your fifth wedding anniversary?"

Mandela laughed, then said, "In our custom, we don't share such things with young ladies like yourself."

It was one of many wonderful moments I have had covering Mandela over the years. During his first trip to the United States, in June 1990, our *NewsHour* team joined with the Council on Foreign Relations, and I moderated a televised town hall meeting at the council's offices in New York, one of Mandela's first extended exposures to viewers in the United States. During the New York meeting he was forthright and charming but still guarded, especially when it came to questions aimed at getting at the interior Madiba—Mandela's clan name, used as a sign of both affection and respect.

My next close encounter with Mandela was on the eve of the first all-race elections in the country, as he was about to take another step on his long walk to freedom. In my last interview with him a few days before he took the oath of office as president of South Africa, he was as generous as ever, becoming the gracious *tata* or grandfather figure when I told him that I would not actually be there to witness this historic moment due to a conflict with my son's graduation from Emory University.

But later in the interview, I glimpsed another side of Mandela: the strength and power that had allowed him to steer his country through the often stormy negotiations that could have plunged the country into civil chaos if not war, but which instead led to the realization of the vision of South Africa Mandela had held in his head and heart for most of his life: a country with a constitution affirming the declaration contained in the ANC Freedom Charter, adopted on June 26, 1955: "South Africa belongs to all who live in it, black and white."

I told Mandela of an interview I had done earlier in the week with F. W. de Klerk, the outgoing president of the country, who had taken the bold step of unbanning Mandela's ANC and releasing him from prison. When I had asked de Klerk what it felt like to be giving up the leadership of the country, he predicted it was only a temporary abdication—that, in fact, he expected to be back in the driver's seat within five years. "A liberation movement will never be able to govern," de Klerk had confidently predicted, and he had gone on to suggest that Mandela's presidency would not be as strong as his had been.[12]

When I repeated his words to Mandela, the soon-to-be president knitted his brow, and his gentle face hardened. One fist was clenched in his lap, and a finger on the other hand jabbed the air as he spoke in a raised voice. "The question of a president being powerful does not depend on the clauses in legislation. You can be powerful and exercise all the power you want without even occupying the position of president, and it's a false idea to think that the power of any individual to influence policy depends on occupying a political position. And I have all the power, legal power, which I need, but I don't solely rely on that. My power of persuasion is sufficient. I have wielded power as a prisoner without occupying any position, and Mr. de Klerk had to recognize that. We have taken decisions and forced him to use his legal powers. The decision was taken by us. . . . We gave him an ultimatum that he must appoint a judicial commission to investigate a question of violence. He must dismiss a certain two ministers. And he came out, and said he would never do that. We embarked on mass action. He was forced to do exactly what he said he would never do. So we have wielded power before we assumed government of the country, and that is how the situation should be examined. It is without any such data for him to say I will not exercise the power that he exercised. It is what the masses of the people decide a president should do. And I am going to be a servant of the masses of the people."[13]

Mandela and his compatriots had acquired this confidence through their moral authority and determined sacrifice. But even though over the years he has opened wider the door on his life in prison, including many of the lighter moments, he doesn't dwell on the pain of his twenty-seven-year ordeal. The effects, though, are increasingly visible, aging notwithstanding—his tall, still proud body slowly bending, the once defiant stride gradually giving way to a slow and lumbering gait painful to him and to others to observe, eyes unable to take the glare of light or the pop of a camera flash as the result of constant exposure to the blazing sun while being forced to dig in a limestone quarry on Robben Island. Few stories have emerged either of the extent of the shared suffering—especially of the younger men sent to prison in their teens and early twenties, such as Saki Macozoma, Moss Ngoasheng, Tokyo Sexwale, Mosiuoa ("Terror") Lekota, Murphy Morobe, and many others who came to be tutored by Mandela and other elders including Walter Sisulu and Ahmed Kathrada, transforming Robben Island into Mandela University. Today, they are a part of the new news of South Africa—Macozoma, Ngoasheng, and Sexwale are top business leaders, Lekota is the minister of defense, and Morobe is the head of communications in the presidency. But like countless other South Africans, they are still not far from the brutal experiences they hold in their memory.

The bitterness of such memories could have resulted in civil conflict during the country's transition from white minority rule. But the creation of the Truth and Reconciliation Commission (TRC) helped avoid this outcome, and its efforts to find truth not told are another example of new news.

The TRC was established in 1995 to compile the most comprehensive list of atrocities of the apartheid era between March 1, 1960, and May 11, 1994. The idea behind it was to give whites, in the main, but also those who took part in armed struggle against the regime, an opportunity to tell the truth about their gross violations of human rights in the name of politics during the apartheid era, in exchange for amnesty—freedom from prosecution. The seventeen commissioners and numerous support staff logged thousands of miles around the country, investigating some thirty-one thousand cases of human rights abuses over the three-year period of the commission's existence. As Alex Boraine, the deputy head of the TRC, has written: "It was a ritual, deeply needed to cleanse a nation. It was a drama. The actors were in the main ordinary people with a powerful story. But this was no brilliantly written play; it was the unvarnished truth in all its starkness."[14]

As I wrote in the introduction to *Country of My Skull*, South African writer Antjie Krog's chronicle of her professional and personal journey through the process:

> Controversy dogged the TRC from the start. There were those who believed that the perpetrators of gross human-rights violations should appear before a court of law, as Nazi war criminals were forced to do at Nuremberg; that, they insisted, was the only possible path to justice. But there were also those who pointed out that it was not a battlefield victory that had produced the end of apartheid, but a settlement negotiated by victims and perpetrators alike; amnesty, they argued, had been a necessary precondition for securing the cooperation of the previous

government and its security forces. The deal was to hold out the promise of amnesty in exchange for the full truth about the past.[15]

To be sure, the commission heard what Allister Sparks, South Africa's premier chronicler of the country's transitions, has called "a cascade of horror."[16] White policemen testified to drugging and killing Sizwe Kondile, a young antiapartheid activist, and burning his body while they drank and told jokes nearby. As Captain Dirk Coetzee described it:

> The burning of a body on an open fire takes seven hours. Whilst that happened, we were drinking and braaing [barbecuing] next to the fire. . . . The fleshier parts of the body take longer . . . that's why we frequently had to turn the buttocks and thighs of Kondile . . . by the morning, we raked through the ashes to see that no piece of bone or teeth was left. Then we all went our own ways.[17]

Black women told of their abuse. Ntombizanele Elsie Zingxondo testified:

> Kruger put paper and a piece of cloth in my mouth. Van der Merwe bound my hands and eyes.
>
> Kruger took off my jersey and my shirt and pulled me up to the desk. One of them took off my bra. They forced me to bend over the open drawer so that one of my breasts would hang in the drawer. They then slammed the drawer shut so that my breast was squashed. They did this three times to each of my breasts. Their actions caused me a lot of pain and my whole body became weak. They also pulled handfuls of hair out of my head.[18]

The TRC also heard of atrocities on the other side: ANC bombings that resulted in the death of innocents; the "necklacing" (putting a burning tire around the neck) of those thought to be collaborating with the apartheid government; Nelson Mandela's then-wife Winnie's involvement in the kidnapping and murder of a fourteen-year-old boy.

But the heaviest burden fell on those at the highest levels of the apartheid apparatus. To sometimes much too small, overcrowded, and overheated rooms around the country, where the panel of eighteen South Africans of various hues sat on either side of Archbishop Tutu, came a parade of top apartheid-era government officials. Most testified that they "didn't know" about the evil deeds being done in their government's name, attributing them to "rogue elements" operating on their own. Telling the truth was the sine qua non of the TRC's contract with the perpetrators, and most didn't honor it. When they purported to tell the truth, most lied.

As *Washington Post* journalist Lynne Duke wrote in her book *Mandela, Mobutu and Me*:

> The people who did these terrible things by and large walked free. Not jailed, not even accused, perhaps sometimes tortured in their own souls, they blended into the woodwork of the new South Africa. Some were in the new police force and the newly reconstituted military. Some were in civilian clothes and retired. Their secrets, and the trail of pain that haunted the nation, constituted a menace to the new democracy.[19]

The debate continues today over whether the TRC's approach was the correct one and about the legacy it has left. It surfaces sometimes on radio talk shows or in the relaxed late-night atmosphere of a private home after dinner and drinks and conversation about more current things. It is not a loud or raucous debate, but it is one often fueled by unrelieved pain.

Many are still seeking reparations. The final codicil to the report of the Truth and Reconciliation Commission recommended a one-time payment to certified victims, and suggested that businesses that were operating during apartheid help pay for these reparations. But the government rejected the TRC's recommendation of a "wealth tax" on businesses, and came down firmly against subsequent lawsuits pursued against companies that did business as usual during apartheid.

These suits were filed in November 2002 by, among others, the Apartheid Debt and Reparations Campaign of Jubilee South Africa, a group aligned with the global Jubilee 2000 coalition of organizations that had been pursuing the cancellation of Third World debt. Acting on behalf of victims of state-sponsored torture, murder, rape, arbitrary detention, and inhumane treatment, the group filed suit against foreign banks and companies that had operated in South Africa during apartheid, accusing them of aiding and abetting the minority white regime in "crimes against humanity." Charles Peter Abrahams, one of its attorneys, explained that the suit was brought in the United States because it was "the only country allowing such litigation."[20]

President Mbeki gave this rationale:

We wish to reiterate that the South African Government is not and will not be party to such litigation.

In addition, we consider it completely unacceptable that matters that are central to the future of our country should be adjudicated in foreign courts which bear no responsibility for the well-being of our country and the observance of the perspective contained in our constitution of the promotion of national reconciliation.

While Government recognises the right of citizens to institute legal action, its own approach is informed by the desire to involve all South Africans, including corporate citizens, in a co-operative and voluntary partnership to reconstruct and develop South African society.[21]

The president's position sparked as much debate as the one-time payment of $3,900 to each TRC-certified victim of apartheid. Some victims happily accepted the offer, but many, such as Onicah Diutwileng, said it wasn't fair. She lamented that apartheid had killed her twenty-five-year-old son, shot him in the head, depriving her of her breadwinner. In her sixties, suffering from high blood pressure and heart problems, she told me she had no way to earn money.

Likewise, Thandiwe Shezi told me she suffered from migraines as a result of the electric shock torture her apartheid tormentors inflicted on her, followed by nearly suffocating her with a plastic bag they placed over her head—this just before four of them took her into another room and raped her. She was then placed in solitary confinement for a year.

"We are not suing them to get money and be rich," she told me, "but we are saying they need to come back and acknowledge the wrongs that they have done in our country and come back and try to redress the problem."[22]

The suit was thrown out by a U.S. district court judge on September 29, 2004, on the grounds that there had been no violation of commercial law. But the litigants appealed, arguing that this was the "strongest case yet in enforcing international norms in respect of behavior of foreign multinational companies."[23]

But the debate over what constitutes closure, if not justice, for the victims of the most extreme apartheid brutality is not likely to end, even if it dies down. It will be fueled by those who may have given up on monetary recompense but who are driven by traditions that demand the dead be honored with proper burial. Most South Africans visit the graves of family members seeking blessing or advice or absolution from the ancestors buried there. So many have abandoned hope of justice. They simply want the bones of their loved ones. But countless victims of apartheid disappeared without a trace and are unlikely ever to be found.[24] Both in TRC testimony and the court case of Wouter Basson (known as "Dr. Death"), the man in charge of Project Coast, the apartheid regime's secret biological and chemical warfare program, details emerged outlining how antiapartheid activists were burned alive, their bones tossed into rivers, or their bodies thrown from planes into the sea.

Frank Chikane, the director general in the office of the president, who presumably supported the Mbeki government's position against the "wealth tax," also has unresolved issues from the apartheid era. He simply wants the truth. In 1989, as general secretary of the South African Council of Churches, Chikane was on his way to the United States via Namibia, which at the time was preparing for its first elections after almost seventy years under South African administration. He checked his bag at the Johannesburg airport and boarded the plane for Namibia. Sometime after arriving there, Chikane remembered, he fell ill: "Your temperature goes high, you feel like throwing out [sic]. Your body begins to tremble and within an hour, I can't pick up my body. It happened fast. By the time they drove me to the hospital, they had to carry me on a stretcher."[25] Chikane said doctors worked for five hours trying to save his life. Stabilized, he was flown back to Johannesburg, recovering only after six days. Not long after, Chikane flew with a delegation to the United States to meet with President George H. W. Bush to discuss the sanctions and disinvestment campaign against South Africa. Prior to the meeting, Chikane again began feeling ill, and went into a public restroom, where he collapsed. He awoke in intensive care. After a third attack, it was finally discovered that Chikane had been the victim of a lethal nerve poison that had been placed in his clothing.

Details of the poisoning emerged at Basson's trial, as did more information about the activities of Project Coast. The scientists there created toxic chemical substances to kill and maim anti-apartheid activists such as Chikane. They harvested the bacterium that causes cholera, laced beer with the bacterium that causes botulism, contaminated soft drinks with *E. coli*, made deadly insecticides and cigarettes and chocolates laced with anthrax, and experimented with potions aimed at making black women sterile.

A former apartheid security agent testified about how two security police told him the poison had to be put on Chikane's underwear after he checked his bags at the Johannesburg airport. He testified he had picked the lock on the suitcase and handed the bag over to two men known as Manie and Gert, although he didn't see them apply the poison. But Basson, who was the brains behind Project Coast and oversaw its activities, was acquitted, and the agents who are believed to have carried out the poisoning remain free.

Chikane, who knows the identity of the two agents, says he's not interested in having them go to jail, though that possibility lies open. "I've made it quite clear before, I have no interest in punishing people," he told me. "There are so many people who were involved. I've been tortured so many times. There are doctors who just didn't take care of you. I'm not sure you want to send them to prison and spend a hundred rands a day to keep them there. That's not going to help this nation. I think what is important for us [is] to know the truth so that we do not have that happen again. I am not a prisoner of the past, but they are prisoners of the past. We don't want people in the new South Africa sitting as prisoners all over here. We want them to come out and be free and I am ready to give them their freedom."[26]

But the perpertrators have not been willing to tell the truth so far. And while the page may turn as Chikane and the others get on with their lives, the final chapter is yet to be written, the book closed on one of the greatest injustices of our time.

Yet however imperfect the process may have been—and Archbishop Tutu, as chair of the TRC and its spiritual and moral compass, is the first to admit its weaknesses—the new news is that South Africa's model of relatively peaceful transition and reconciliation is being used as a model in societies around the African continent, including Nigeria and Rwanda, as well as other parts of the world. Sudan's prime minister told South Africa's *Mail and Guardian* newspaper in 2005 that Sudan would "seek Pretoria's official intervention" in helping that country put itself back together after twenty-one years of a bruising conflict between the north and the south.[27]

The kind of vigorous activism that helped end apartheid has mostly died out, taking life out of much of civil society. Most international donors who helped fund the organizations of anti-apartheid activists declared victory in 1994 when apartheid officially ended, and they closed their checkbooks and went home. Apartheid's legacy left many unresolved problems, but it has taken a while for new local civic groups to form and find support. Yet civil society is slowly regrouping—now around issues involving gender, land, housing, health, and other basic services. In mid-2005, some of the country's black townships erupted in street riots over the lack of such necessities as water and electricity, and the concern within the country was that if the unrest continued, it could threaten the still-young democracy. The violence abated, but not the simmering discontent, which many believe feeds the disenchantment with South Africa's policy of what it calls "black economic empowerment." So far, South Africa's blacks have not seen that empowerment trickle down to their shacks in still segregated townships, where nothing has changed.

One of the most successful groups in the new South Africa so far has been organized around HIV/AIDS. South Africa has the highest number of people living with HIV in the world, more than five million. HIV-related deaths among young people fifteen years of age and older increased by 62 percent from 1997 to 2002. And AIDS-related deaths account for 30 percent of all deaths nationwide, according to the South African Medical Research Council. Moreover, the adult prevalence of HIV in South Africa soared from less than 1 percent in 1990 to almost 25 percent by 2000, according to the United Nations.[28]

The AIDS activist group Treatment Action Campaign (TAC), which estimates an average of six hundred new infections per day, has used the old tactics of street demonstrations as well as court challenges to pressure the government to move faster on the AIDS pandemic. The courts ruled in TAC's favor, requiring the government to provide nevirapine, a drug that dramatically reduces mother-to-child transmission of HIV during birth, and later TAC's pressure led to the government's providing antiretroviral drugs free to all who need them.

Although I have been in many clinics that treat people living with HIV, I continue to be amazed each time by what I see. The clients are mostly female and young, beautiful girls often wearing the latest fashion blue jeans and sassy tops and sporting the latest hair styles. They could be auditioning for a magazine ad or a spot on one of the many popular TV soaps. They are at once giggly and flirty and sometimes shy with strangers, like girls their age all over the world. Nothing would tell you they were infected with HIV, unless they have—as many do—a child whose half-closed eyelids, drooling, and telltale rashes point to the presence of AIDS.

I visited one clinic near Johannesburg, called the Tuesday Clinic to avoid the dreaded A-word. The scene made me wonder about the future of the nation, with so many of its potential mothers infected. But while most of the patients are young girls, there are also old grannies and middle-aged aunties, often innocent victims of unfaithful partners who know but don't tell and who still insist on having sex "skin to skin." Many of the men die, leaving nothing to support the women and the children they've left behind.

Former president Nelson Mandela, who has acknowledged that his government did little to contain the scourge, has become one of the most visible public figures to take on the problem, which claimed his only surviving son in 2005. The former president, who is the most revered person in the country, and a handful of others have tried to convince a stigma-wary public that AIDS is like any other disease. But even from an icon such as Mandela, the plea has fallen mostly on deaf ears, with many still arguing there is no such thing as AIDS, even when their own bodies are telling them differently. It's called denial, and it has led to incalculable death rates, easily numbering in the tens of thousands. One newspaper report told of South Africans stealing into hospitals in the dark of night to avoid being seen by anyone who might recognize them.[29] Activists and even mainstream medical practitioners and others blame much of this on South Africa's current president, Thabo Mbeki, who has questioned whether HIV causes AIDS, bolstering the case of so-called AIDS dissidents.

There is no one position among AIDS dissidents. Some argue that the virus that causes AIDS has never been isolated; others claim that it doesn't exist at all. Yet another group holds that AIDS is a concoction of the pharmaceutical industry aimed at making a profit, while some argue AIDS is a collection of old diseases such as TB that are affected by the environment of poverty and malnutrition and that together they compromise the immune system. Mbeki himself has never made an explicit statement denying that HIV causes AIDS, but he has questioned how a single virus can cause a syndrome.

In recent years, he has generally refrained from public comment on the science of HIV/AIDS, leaving it to his minister of health, Manto Tshabalala Msimang, to make statements questioning the impact of antiretroviral therapy and instead promoting nutrition, especially the use of olive oil, garlic, and beetroot, as being as effective as antiretrovirals. Many see the minister, a medical doctor who is often referred to as "Dr. Garlic," as a surrogate for the president, and all of this has clearly affected perceptions of South Africa, especially in the United States, where many associate Mbeki with what they see as the "wacky" AIDS dissidents. The issue has threatened to overshadow his otherwise keen intellect and significant achievements on the continent.

Part of Mbeki's attitude about AIDS stems from his belief that AIDS has gotten a disproportionate share of attention, given that the overarching problem in South Africa and on the African continent is poverty, and that addressing the poverty issue comprehensively and with urgency will lead to a more effective response not just to AIDS but to all of the debilitating and deadly diseases threatening the recovery of the continent, including malaria, heart disease, diabetes, diarrheal diseases, and non-AIDS-related tuberculosis. But it is clear that his deep-rooted concerns about racism form much of the core of his thinking. In a heated parliamentary exchange with opposition members of Parliament, who accused him of being an "AIDS denialist," Mbeki said he would not keep quiet while "others whose minds have been corrupted by the disease of racism accuse us, the black people of South Africa . . . [of] being, by virtue of our Africanness and skin colour, lazy, liars, foul-smelling, diseased, corrupt, violent, amoral, sexually depraved, animalistic, savage and rapist."[30] Mbeki's characterization brings to mind the term "*swaart gevaar*," Afrikaans for "black hordes," used by the apartheid regime when rallying the country's whites against the antiapartheid activists threatening to overrun them and their self-presumed God-given right to rule.

Mbeki cited his earlier criticism of AIDS activist Charlene Smith and UNAIDS's Kathleen Cravero, who, he said,

> had written that "our cultures, religion and social norms as Africans condition us to be rampant sexual beasts, unable to control our urges, unable to keep our legs crossed, unable to keep it in our pants."
>
> "These were the rapists the Honourable [Democratic Alliance member of parliament Ryan] Coetzee says that in large part account for the spread of HIV in the country."
>
> Mbeki said he prayed that sooner rather than later, South Africans of all races "will dare to drag racism from the hushed conversations and murmurs and silences into the arena of public discussion."[31]

Coetzee criticized Mbeki for "rant[ing] on about the stereotypes of black people that he believes whites harbour" and said Mbeki had scorned an opportunity to redeem himself and his government on AIDS. 'The question is whether a person who cannot lead the country on an issue as central and critical as HIV/Aids is the right person to lead the country at all."[32]

*Washington Post* reporter Jon Jeter wrote an article that provided one of the most insightful analyses aimed at "decoding South Africa's ineffectual official response to its most dire heath crisis." His lengthy piece posited that "the government's failure to deal with AIDS jeopardized practically everything the country has achieved since the end of oppressive white rule." Jeter found the issue complicated, but all roads of his inquiry led him to "the raw and deep wound left by the racial caste system of apartheid."

After decades of seeing friends and relatives jailed, poisoned and even sterilized by whites, the ANC shut clinics that could have been useful in treating and counseling patients infected with HIV, largely because the facilities were heavily staffed by white doctors, according to people involved in AIDS policy. After negotiating an uneasy co-existence with the white minority, the new leaders' initial efforts to address the epidemic were slowed and even sabotaged by white civil servants inherited from the apartheid era.

And when medical experts warned them that a home-grown vaccine was worthless, leaders from the president down plowed quixotically ahead. Those involved in the effort say they were convinced that they could redeem the indignities, insults and stereotypes that Africans had endured at the hands of whites by discovering a miracle vaccine for a disease that not even the West could cure.

"I don't think anyone can give a simple explanation for why our AIDS program has failed," said Morna Cornell, director of the AIDS Consortium, a nonprofit counseling project. "But the race issue is huge. It's like we eliminated apartheid but it left behind this huge wall that none of us knew how to tear down or get around."[33]

Jeter goes on:

The ANC's return to open politics coincided with a seismic shift in the spread of HIV. Largely isolated to white, gay men when it first appeared in the country in the early 1980s, the virus had by 1990 begun affecting primarily black heterosexuals.

"It was doubly stigmatized," said Mark Gevisser, a South African journalist who is writing a biography of Mbeki. "It went from being the 'Gay Plague' to the 'Black Death' and it really reinforced the stereotype of the super sexualized, irresponsible black male. This is the stigma that the exiles came home to."

As the ANC and then-ruling National Party engaged in tense negotiations for a transition to majority rule, the apartheid regime used fear of AIDS to undermine the popularity of their adversary. Fliers with crude depictions of black men began to appear in the black townships, warning that virus-carrying exiles were importing HIV to the country.

"That definitely put us on the defensive," said Smuts Ngonyama, an ANC spokesman. "We, on the one hand, understood that this was a disease that we needed to deal with. But we also resented the National Party's demonization of us as promiscuous . . . and terrorists bringing death and disease home to our people. They were aggressively selling this stigma so that we couldn't stand on the moral high ground. People would say to us: 'You know, I'm just not sure about the ANC.' "[34]

Even Glenda Gray, a senior researcher in the maternity ward of Chris Hani Baragwanath Hospital in Soweto, one of the largest black medical centers in the world, which today is close to buckling under the strain of AIDS patients, allowed that the country's racist past has had an effect on fighting the AIDS battle. She told Jeter: "I don't know how you get a national AIDS program to work when you've inherited a civil service that you don't trust and that doesn't trust you and wants to stick it to you at every turn." And Jeter pointed out that Mandela only spoke publicly about AIDS for the first time three years into his five-year term and that his first budget included only $15 million for a national AIDS campaign, rather than the $64 million proposed by an AIDS panel assembled by the ANC.[35]

But Mbeki defended his government's performance, telling me in an interview that his government spends more on AIDS than any other government on the continent, allocating in 2003 the equivalent of about U.S. $2 billion over the following three years.[36]

The government also began dispensing free antiretroviral drugs, putting them into the hands of the poor for the first time, and estimated that between 2003 and 2010 the lives of some 1.7 million South Africans would be saved as a result. There is no cure for AIDS, but despite side effects in some patients, these drugs have established an impressive record in restoring health and prolonging life.

The program had a slow rollout, however, in part due to the lack of trained personnel to administer the drugs and a lack of adequately equipped sites, especially in rural areas. The national plan called for a rollout of antiretrovirals to 53,000 patients by March 2005, but by April of that year they had fallen short, with only 43,000 patients having received the drugs. At the same time, UNAIDS reported that almost 900,000 people actually needed the drugs.[37] Moreover, many who are receiving them are getting them too late, and their deaths cause even more skepticism among an already confused public.

President Mbeki fueled criticism of his response to the crisis when, on a visit to the United States in 2003, he told a *Washington Post* reporter he didn't know of anyone who had died of AIDS.[38] Most found that hard to understand, even if one adopts the strictest medical definition (as Mbeki might have been doing given his predisposition to intellectual precision) that one dies not from AIDS but from complications arising from a compromised immune system, such as tuberculosis or pneumonia. Also, there was widespread publicity given to the death from AIDS of Mbeki's former spokesperson, Parks Mankahlana, and the former head of the African National Congress Youth League, Peter Mokaba. In fact, most people living in South Africa have lost friends, relatives, acquaintances, co-workers, or employees to AIDS complications.

Opposition leader Mangosuthu Buthelezi, a descendent of royalty, antiapartheid campaigner, former cabinet member, and leader of the Zulu-based Inkatha Freedom Party, lost a son and a daughter to AIDS within months of each other in 2004. He said, "If I was at the helm, I would regard HIV and AIDS as our number one priority because we can talk about a better life for all and all the things we dream up for our children, but if they are being decimated, as the case is, by this pandemic, who are we doing those things for?"[39]

As a journalist, I have covered many stories about AIDS and talked with many of its victims, in various stages of the disease. But I also have close friends and associates who have family members who are suffering from the disease's complications or who died of them. One of those was Nomsa, whom I became close to after doing a story on AIDS orphans. Following the death of her mother, her stepfather "took her for his wife," in the words of Trudy Howell, the head of the orphanage where the girl was living. At the time, Nomsa was six. Her stepfather infected her with HIV.

When I met Nomsa, she was thin, shy, and very sick. It was before the government began providing free antiretroviral drugs, and Howell and the nurse caring for Nomsa, Deborah Kodisang, kept saying that if only they could find the money for the drugs, they were sure they could save the girl.

In time, I helped organize funds to buy the drugs, and they did indeed save Nomsa. She gained weight, her spirits soared, and she even became "cheeky," as South Africans describe someone with a sassy attitude. She was able to return to school—a mixed blessing in the end, for it was there that she contracted chicken pox, which proved too much for her immune system, already compromised during her long wait for antiretrovirals. After putting up a brave fight, she died at age twelve.

In a country urgently trying to move beyond apartheid, it is proving difficult to escape it as a point of reference, even on AIDS. One of the country's staunchest antiapartheid stalwarts and moral leaders, Archbishop Desmond Tutu, has called AIDS "the new apartheid," meaning still another relentless oppression denying its victims the basic rights of health and human dignity.

It would be difficult to measure the extent to which perceptions about HIV's impact on South Africa have affected international investment in the country. Officially, the unemployment rate stands close to 30 percent, with the majority lacking education and skills—already an uninviting prospect for investors. Add to that the perception that the workforce is sick and dying, and interest in the country as an investment destination diminishes even further.

But even amid all the bad news there is new news. Strong growth in the domestic economy "has highlighted attractive investment opportunities," according to financial analyst Marisa Fassler of JPMorgan Chase Bank, and may offset some of the negative perceptions from AIDS.[40] Moreover, some major companies are stepping up and putting in place programs aimed at keeping their workforce healthier longer. Because of their mobility and work that takes them far away from home for long periods, men working in the mines—particularly the gold mines—have some of the highest HIV infection rates in the country. The London-based mining corporation Anglo

American—the biggest company operating in South Africa—reports seeing vast improvements in the health of its employees following the introduction of comprehensive HIV programs that encourage workers to find out their HIV status and then provide counseling and treatment. For those ill enough, the company provides antiretroviral therapy.

Dr. Brian Brink, a senior vice president for health at Anglo American who was instrumental in developing the company's approach, told me in 2005: "Before, people feared AIDS. They feared stigma. They feared discrimination, but now with a good treatment program, people understand it. The fear of the disease, the stigma, the discrimination, it all disappears into the background. We've come out of the valley of the shadow of death and [are looking] at a whole new vista of inspiration. We haven't got there but we can see the way. I know that given the right leadership, we can do it.

"What's really exciting is the HIV prevalence rate is exactly the same as last year, which means no new infections, no one is getting sick and no one is dying."[41]

At the same time, Brink acknowledged that Anglo American's program is far from perfect. He estimated that some 9,000 of the company's 34,000 workers were probably infected, with only 3,000 having come forward to date to participate in the company's initiative. Moreover, the Anglo American program, like most others, does not cover workers' family members, though for now those individuals have recourse to the government's provision of free antiretroviral therapy for all who need it—provided there are trained staff and sufficient infrastructure.

The remaining challenges are enormous—not least the millions of children orphaned by AIDS. The sheer number of AIDS orphans is ripping apart the social fabric of the extended family, one of the fundamentals of African society and culture. Surviving relatives who are willing to care for these children are overwhelmed—especially grandmothers, who often have lost more than one adult child to the virus and have taken on responsibility for the grandchildren.

I have sat with many such women around their mud-and-thatch rondavels as the littlest ones played, sometimes naked in the dirt, as the school-age ones sat idly by, their *gogo* (an older relative) unable to afford the fees and uniforms needed for them to go to school.

I have also met young people such as Wendy Bawelele Zulu, who lost both parents to AIDS and was taking care of her siblings, the youngest of whom was two. My cameraperson, Cynde Strand, captured her as she rose before dawn, lit a fire in their one-room wattle-and-daub hut, boiled water and made porridge, then woke the younger children and prepared them for school. When all was done, she got ready to go to her own school, where she was in seventh grade.

Though Brink and others are unhappy about such situations and the slow implementation of the government's comprehensive program, they argue that AIDS is now embedded in a human rights framework and that the law mandating no discrimination against HIV-positive individuals and ensuring their confidentiality and rights is "excellent stuff." Furthermore, they believe that such a policy framework will ultimately lead to an effective response.

"It's like the destruction of the pillars of apartheid," Brink said. "Many had some doubts as to whether it was real and whether we would see a true establishment of democratic rule, majority rule, in South Africa. But in time this was an irreversible change. What we see today is a society completely transformed, and it is the same with the policy commitment to AIDS. It is irreversible."[42]

The AIDS pandemic has cast a long, dark shadow over South Africa's "miracle," from the coal face to the classroom, hospital corridors and the corridors of power. But the new news is found in the gains that have been made and in the optimism of those who are facing up to the challenge and achieving small victories.

Apartheid has been legally dead for more than ten years, and while it will take a lot longer than that to untangle the tentacles of its white supremacist legacy, the South African government has been systematic in its efforts to put in place legislation and policies aimed at making sure this untangling happens at every layer of society.

Having lived through the rancorous U.S. debate over affirmative action, I find it fascinating to see how differently a country with a black-led government deals with issues of race and redress. In South Africa, affirmative action is not a dirty word; it's government policy.

In explaining the country's "unapologetic affirmative action," South African Constitutional Court justice Yvonne Mokgoro told a symposium at the University of Michigan that the country's constitution "sets standards for all public action, programs and policy. . . . Our courts do not need to grapple with whether affirmative action is permissible or not. . . . If it can be justified, it is not unfair, therefore it is lawful."[43]

The government's efforts to establish what Mokgoro calls "substantive equality" has led to policies that affect every segment of society, including the workplace, where employment equity and the policy of black economic empowerment are holding out the promise of the most radical economic transformation in recent times, aimed at reversing generations of policies designed specifically to keep a whole race of people outside the economic mainstream.

Nowhere is the effort to make up for past exclusion more dramatic (and important, given the woeful lack of skilled blacks in the society) than at universities across the country. I visited the University of Cape Town's medical school, where the black dean recalled that during apartheid he was one of a handful of black students admitted, but wasn't allowed to enter a room with white cadavers, and could only examine their remains if they were enclosed in a jar. Now the school has a vigorous affirmative action program, accepting black students with lower grades than whites as a way of counterbalancing the obstacles black students had to overcome over the years to get to the university's front door.

In 2004, I followed one of these young students, twenty-two-year-old Sicelo Bangani, in his crisp white lab coat from the bedside of a patient, where he confidently made an assessment of her medical condition, to the poor rural township where he grew up, some twenty-three hours and a world away. His home was in the Transkei, home to Nelson Mandela and the Xhosa people—a vast portion of land eight hundred miles east of Cape Town, described by Mandela as "a beautiful country of rolling hills, fertile valleys, and a thousand rivers and streams, which keep the landscape green, even in winter."[44]

But the Transkei is as poor as it is beautiful. Sicelo grew up there as a herd boy, more used to cows than computers. When we arrived on a bright, sunny day, I could see in my mind's eye my own journey to the front door of the University of Georgia, which had never admitted a black student in its 176-year history. I could see my long walk from my home in the small town of Covington, Georgia, to the Washington Street School, the all-black elementary school that suffered mightily from the white administration's separate and unequal distribution of funds, which meant that we had to study from the hand-me-down textbooks from the white schools (often with pages missing) and their other secondhand offerings.

Sicelo took me to his school, a few modest concrete buildings with tin roofs. Inside, in the stifling heat, students in their neat little uniforms, sometimes fifty or more in a class, sat three and four to the few small desks available.

Sicelo told me that when he was getting ready to study for the medical school entrance examinations, none of his teachers was qualified to teach advanced math and science. A sympathetic vice principal obtained some books and a study guide for him, and he went forward on his own. I also identified with that, harking once again back to my growing up in a segregated society, where, though blacks were regarded as second-class and inferior by whites, our black teachers passed on something no law could restrict: a first-class sense of ourselves.

Like many of the students in previously predominantly white schools, Sicelo had battled to keep up when he first got to the university. "Academically," he said, "I really struggled at first. Not to do with my level of intelligence or something like that, but really with the technology. I wasn't used to that kind of stuff. And I would be shocked to even hold a microscope!"[45]

The University of Cape Town provided remedial sessions and tutors, and eventually Sicelo was able to perform considerably above acceptable levels. Part of his motivation was his desire to return to the Transkei and offer the kind of basic health care services that for now are in short supply. He told me: "Even with their superior grades, this is something that would never occur to white students. They wouldn't come here."[46]

Even more important, perhaps, Sicelo's success will send a message to the young students still stuck in those hot, poorly ventilated classrooms, sitting with their knees scraping against their rusty desks, that they too can make it to a place they once never dared dream of.

The next big challenge is ensuring more successful outcomes at universities such as the University of Cape Town and Johannesburg's prestigious University of the Witwatersrand, where the student body has gone from majority white to majority black since the end of apartheid. Of all the countries on the continent, South Africa has the greatest chance of entering the global economy as a serious player. One of its biggest challenges is arming its young people with the tools to help the country sustain itself in a global arena that has no affirmative action.

It is a challenge that will require creativity and flexibility, but the new news is that black students who once abandoned their studies, taking to the streets and putting their bodies on the line to end apartheid, are now back—some on campuses they could never have set foot on before, at least not as students. And they are back with a vengeance to claim a basic right enshrined in the country's new constitution—the right to education.

More young blacks are coming into the educational arena, but most still come from poor families, barely able to afford food, rent, and clothes, much less the cost of a college education. As a result, universities across the country are now facing a financial crisis, having trouble providing funds for the dramatic increase in their student bodies. The University of the Witwatersrand was racked by student riots in 2004, when it cut in half financial aid to needy students. Among the three thousand protesters were students such as third-year BA student Marubini Malaudzi, twenty-one, who told a newspaper reporter she "skips breakfast and lunch but eats supper at the University residence," saving the equivalent of some $300 per year. But, she said, with the cut in her financial aid and a jobless mother living in a rural township, she won't be coming back for her final year.[47] The university's move was prompted by the huge increase in students needing assistance, up from 600 the previous year to over 3,000. As a result, the entering freshman class dropped to 2,400 from 3,500 the year before. Subsequently, in consultation with the Student Representative Council, an agreement was reached to allocate aid to returning students first, and to limit financial aid for new students to those whose families were unable to contribute anything toward their tuition, in order "to ensure that students with academic potential are given access and the best possible chance to succeed."[48] This action came as the state also froze the number of students it would subsidize for the 2005 year.

The huge pool of previously disadvantaged poor students eager for an education has led to some innovative programs, such as the country's first free university, CIDA (Community and Individual Development Association), a thriving enterprise in the inner city, focusing on business and management. The school has many unique features. Every student from a disadvantaged background is on a scholarship. Moreover, it is a requirement that students share with the community the education and skills they gain. They are also required to help maintain the institution's high-rise building and grow some of their own food in its rooftop garden. There are few permanent faculty members, with most lecturers borrowed from the banking and financial institutions that will ultimately benefit most from a well-trained cadre of students in the field.

CIDA's founder, former investment banker Taddy Bletcher, sees his institution as helping to make up for past discrimination in a fundamental way:

> CIDA City Campus is a catalyst for providing more open access to relevant tertiary education as a fundamental driver for wealth creation. The graduates from this year alone will generate between R800 million (roughly $120 million US) to R2 billion (roughly $300 million US) in income over the course of their working careers. This is 100 times more than the cost of the investment in their education. There is no finer return on investment than every single rand spent in investing in economically relevant higher education and entrepreneurial opportunity. These earn-

ings will go directly into the hands of historically disadvantaged families.[49]

CIDA, like most institutions of higher learning in South Africa, is challenged to make up for generations of separate and unequal education that can still be seen in the schools of black townships today. Many if not most of them suffer from a lack of books, as well as modern educational tools such as computers. Few have science labs where students can conduct practical experiments. Little has changed since the days when a university science teacher I once interviewed told me he'd gotten all the way to college only reading about laboratory experiments, never conducting one himself because there were no laboratories.

I visited one of those schools in 2002, as South African Mark Shuttleworth, a wealthy young businessman, was about to become the first "Afronaut" launched into space. At the last minute —I think when my CNN crew called to ask about coming— a small television set was hastily rigged up on a rusty cabinet in the front of the tiny room that was the library, and some fifty students crammed in between the shelves with few books to watch this historic moment. Few others around the country were so lucky. And yet here, as elsewhere around the country, the desire for education is strong, and committed teachers are managing to produce some high achievers by sheer determination, commitment, and will.

And that is part of the South African miracle—that for all the perils that lie ahead, young people in South Africa do now have the space to dream. To be sure, it's early days—a fact about which those of us who make judgments and take measurements need to be constantly reminded.

Having gained political power and consolidated it with a two-thirds majority in the election of 2004, the black-led government is taking bold steps to crack the solid wall of white control over the economy. "To build a unified nation based on equality and justice," Mbeki has told the nation, "we must ensure that the economy is in the hands of all our people."[50]

To that end, the government has instituted policies aimed at bringing greater numbers of blacks into the workplace and creating a black middle class. In 2004, Parliament passed the Black Economic Empowerment Act, laying out a government strategy for broad-based black participation in the economy through restructuring state-owned assets, instituting preferential procurement from black-owned firms, and encouraging companies to sell ownership shares to black investors, train more black workers, and promote more black managers. Charters have been developed to set goals and timetables in most sectors of the economy, including mining, petroleum, maritime, financial services, and winemaking. To take the last of these as an example, less than 1 percent of wine-producing companies are owned by blacks, according to the South African Wine Industry Trust, but the wine charter is targeting 10 to 15 percent black ownership in five years.

A government scorecard will evaluate the performance of companies, holding out carrots: government's tremendous buying power of some $20 billion a year, and preferential treatment to those companies that comply with the goals of black economic empowerment (BEE). The stick for not getting with the program: no government business, and public opprobrium.

The first of these charters to go into effect was mining in October 2002. It called for 26 percent black ownership within ten years. On the day it was adopted, the country's minister of minerals and energy, Pumzile Mlambo-Ngcuka, called it "probably one of the brightest days in the history of transformation." (Mlambo-Ngcuka was subsequently elevated to deputy president in 2005, becoming the first woman to hold the post.)

The implementation of BEE policy has drawn criticism from a variety of sources, with predominantly white opposition parties calling it "reverse racism" and others calling it "crony capitalism." The president has responded that "certain outcomes are fundamental to the very being of the ANC and, therefore, our government." Other criticisms have come as warnings that uncertainty over BEE's ultimate requirements may have a negative effect on foreign direct investment. A 2005 survey by Ernst and Young warned that government needed to clarify its empowerment rules, and cautioned that companies are worried that the charters will be "revisited" by the government, "resulting in further dilution of their shareholdings."[51]

Though the government has embarked on a program of privatizing state-controlled industries, such as telecommunications, this is a long way from the nationalization that was feared back in 1994, as a government that was perceived as left-leaning came to power. (The African National Congress has been described as "a broad church," embracing members from the South African Communist Party, the labor union movement, and civic organizations, among others.) In fact, postapartheid South Africa has drawn plaudits from the international community for its sound economic management, which has reduced the national debt from 48 percent of GDP in 1997 to some 37 percent of GDP in 2003–4. With a budget deficit down to 3 percent of GDP by 2005, the country has experienced the longest period of uninterrupted growth in half a century.

In 2004, black economic empowerment deals reached an estimated R80 billion (roughly a little over $13 billion US), according to Mandisi Mpahlwa, minister of trade and industry, surpassing deals of some R21 billion (roughly $38 million US) in both 1998 and 2003 fueled by black empowerment charters. But there has been widespread criticism of "crony capitalism"—"the overwhelming impression is of well-intentioned economic reorganization drifting toward crony capitalism," the Johannesburg-based *Mail and Guardian* newspaper has editorialized.[52]

Mpahlwa acknowledged that nearly three-quarters of the deals in 2004 had involved at least one of the top six BEE consortiums, headed by the country's most prominent black businessmen. This concentration added weight to the concerns voiced by such critics as Nobel Peace Prize laureate Archbishop Desmond Tutu, who has argued that BEE is not broad-based enough, sharpening the debate over how best to ensure that BEE benefits as many as possible.

No one has been more vocal in his criticisms of BEE than Moeletsi Mbeki, who is the president's brother but not always his ideological soul mate. On one hand, Moeletsi Mbeki, an engineer by training and an entrepreneur, argues that black economic empowerment is a strategy designed in part by corporations aimed at protecting their "privileged position." "In order for the wrongdoer to be able to pay reparations," he told me, "the wrongdoer has to maintain his privileged position so that he can pay reparations. This is the principle of fattening the goose that lays the golden egg. What this means is that the corporations that were allegedly responsible for victimizing the previously disadvantaged individuals must not be transformed beyond putting a few black individuals in their upper echelon."

On the other hand, Mbeki also told me that "the black elite does not see itself as producers. They therefore do not envisage themselves as entrepreneurs who can start and manage new enterprises. At best they see themselves as joining existing enterprises which process is to be facilitated by the disruptive state through reparations inspired legislation."[53]

The criticism that BEE is enriching a few politically connected blacks in deals that do not generate wealth beyond themselves is not accepted by either government or powerful businesspeople. While government officials acknowledged that their BEE policy needs a much more broad-based approach, officials such as Lionel October, of the Department of Trade and Industry, argue that the private sector "has now bought in to it" and that they will help expand the base by being "more inclusive" in their deals. October noted that huge corporations such as mining giant DeBeers and the insurance firm Old Mutual included more women's groups in their deals and are making financing available to rural areas, as well as committing themselves to investing in infrastructure in rural areas.

At the same time, October defended the deals he argues have created a black middle and business class. "During apartheid," he told me, "there was a black professional class, but they didn't generate wealth. They were [even] excluded from owning property. Now, we had to start somewhere. In the early generation of deals, we needed big names, not least because of the publicity the deals would draw, which encouraged the white businesses to go forward. But the good public outcry over [the concentration of deals in the hands of a few well-connected black businessmen] now for the first time has people moving beyond the superstars." October said the government's procurement has all been done with small business and will continue to be as it concentrates on accelerating the process of wealth creation.

He pointed to a R1 billion (about $166,000 US) program instituted by the state-owned Industrial Development Corporation (IDC) in November 2005 and aimed at promoting small business investment, encouraging black economic empowerment, and creating jobs. The IDC would provide low-interest loans with the goal of encouraging investment in labor-intensive projects.

"This is not the old social engineering," he said. "We are going to change the face of the South African economy."[54]

Saki Macozoma, who as a teenager served time on Robben Island with Nelson Mandela and who serves on the all-powerful

ANC National Executive Committee, is among the business elite who take issue with critics such as Moeletsi Mbeki. Macozoma negotiated a BEE deal with Standard Bank, the country's largest, in which the bank sold a 10 percent stake to a group of black participants, including Safika Holdings (Macozoma's company) and Millennium Consolidated Investments (founded by former ANC activist Cyril Ramaphosa); managers' trusts that include 2,500 current and future black managers of the bank; and a community trust.

Said Macozoma:

> It seems that what they seem to be saying is that we don't merit what we are achieving in this society, and that in fact the only reason why we are in positions we are is because we are politically connected and that seems to be the only determinant for how we are advancing in society. We think they are wrong for a number of factors. Firstly, the majority of people, of enterprising people, in this society naturally and necessarily were involved in the liberation struggle. If they had not done so, we would not have won the liberation struggle, so it is natural that those people will migrate from the liberation struggle into the rest of the economy into the rest of society. . . . We are not using political office to get into positions of power and influence; we are using our own natural abilities and attributes and connections in the society that recognizes some of the attributes that we have, and most of us in fact have served the society in many ways.
>
> The fact of the matter is that if all of us stay in the political arena and start handling and jostling about political positions, what we would have in society is political instability, and the reason why many countries on this continent, on the African continent, have difficulty advancing

democracy [is] because there are no alternative places where other individuals can go to and be recognized for their leadership qualities other than government. . . .

Now what we have done in this particular deal is we have aligned the interest of the entrepreneurs with the black employees, but also have made sure that we have worked on the white employees because we don't want the white employees to feel unloved and irrelevant because there's no bank without them either. At the end of the day we are hoping to come up with a truly representative South African bank.[55]

Reg Romney, executive director of the BusinessMap Foundation, a research organization monitoring South African business, argued that BEE critics are not appreciating the time it takes for radical economic reorganization schemes to take root. He pointed to the self-empowerment drive of Afrikaners, known as Help Nekaar, that started as a way to raise funds to pay fines imposed by the British after their 1902 victory in the Boer War. He recalled that it "took some seventy years before it resulted in the accumulation of capital."

Moreover, Romney argued that while BEE so far was "disappointing in that it hasn't yet created entrepreneurial activity, the creation of black businesspeople to amass capital" is a necessary first step toward deracialization of the economy. That many of these black businesspeople are coming from government or are in some way connected to the ruling ANC, he insists, must be seen in light of their being the people with "skills and education and the connections necessary in business."[56]

As the debate over BEE continues, a major challenge for the government remains how to create a broad-based black middle class without destabilizing an economy that has benefited from the government's widely praised economic management, which has ranged from middle of the road to conservative. In July 2002 the government suffered from the leak of a draft of the mining charter calling for 51 percent black ownership. This created an uproar, spawning fears of nationalization and sending mining houses into a tizzy—especially those listed on international stock exchanges, whose share prices plunged. Negative perceptions of the country soared. Intense negotiations between the government, the mining companies, the unions, and other stakeholders resulted in a final document that everyone could live with.

Meanwhile, the government continues to tinker with its BEE policy, making adjustments shaped by realities on the ground. One such adjustment involved new cabinet-approved codes of good practice that encourage companies "to enter into deals with groups that are not necessarily 100 percent black-owned." As the Johannesburg newspaper *Business Day* newspaper reported, "The change has been introduced to remove the disincentive that tends to discourage companies from dealing with 'mixed' entities, which are often essential to provide black entrepreneurs with finance."[57]

Meanwhile, the implementation of policies aimed at employment equity in the workplace over the past decade appears to have had a dramatic effect on the economic status of black Africans, with the number of black households in the high-middle and high income groups increasing by 368 percent between 1998 and 2004, to 440,000, while the number of white households in those groups rose 16 percent, to 642,000.[58] According to Helgard Van Wyk, an economist with the University of South Africa's Bureau of Market Research, this represents a shift in the South African economy, indicating an emerging black middle class. Moreover, close to 3 million working-class South Africans have escaped poverty and moved into the lower middle class. In one of the more dramatic developments, some 1.6 million of those 3 million are women.[59]

At the same time, President Mbeki has acknowledged that the government has not done enough to assist women's advancement into the economy. To that end, in 2005 he established the Presidential Women's Working Group to help women move "from the bottom of the pile." "Most women are still illiterate and victims of violence," he said at a meeting of women entrepreneurs.[60]

Women make up some 52 percent of South Africa's adult population and 41 percent of the workforce, but the top forty companies on the Johannesburg stock exchange are all headed by men, and there are only seven female CEOs in the 364 companies listed on the exchange.[61] Still, black women have made strides into the economy, albeit via the public sector, where they hold positions as CEOs and board members of many parastatals.

"As a nation, we are responding to the skills deficit experienced by other parts of the world, because our democracy acknowledges women's potential, which has remained undervalued and underutilized for many years," said Wendy Luhabe, a founder of Wiphold, a multimillion-dollar enterprise that was the first women's investment group in South Africa. "I am convinced that South Africa will be the first country to demonstrate to the rest of the world what women are capable of."[62]

Bringing blacks into the economic mainstream is not only a remedy for past exclusion and discrimination. It also looks to the future, for broadening the still small South African consumer base will provide a greater lure to foreign investors. The fastest-growing groups in the lower middle class, for example —telephone operators, shop cashiers, semiskilled workers, security guards, junior police officers, and students—have a collective buying power of some R160 billion, or more than U.S. $26 billion.[63]

And while the black middle class is still relatively small, it is by no means invisible, especially the young middle- to upper-middle-class black professionals who are newly financially independent, with money to spend. Their car of choice: a BMW, sold to them by one of their own. Thirty-four-year-old Ciko Thomas owns a BMW dealership in downtown Johannesburg and is doing a rushing business. Of his BMW-purchasing peers, he said: "They've got needs to express themselves, physically, tangibly." Thomas attributes this new development to post-apartheid education levels and "subsequently those educated people being absorbed into the workplace, which frees up money for them to spend on luxury things like cars, especially BMWs."[64]

Upwardly mobile young blacks such as Thomas and his customers have drawn criticism for their sometimes conspicuous consumption, which some see as turning their backs on the continuing struggle to expand freedom's promise beyond the still small group that has gotten its foot in the door economically. But Thomas, who remembers the apartheid era, replied that while he understood the frustration that leads to such criticism, he didn't accept it. "I think we're fighting a different social and political battle," he said in the bright and busy showroom of his dealership. "And I think you're seeing a society that's building itself in different ways and the economic building imperative is upon a lot of black people who historically apartheid has denied a lot of things. I think it's a bit dangerous to say we don't have a social conscience. I think a lot of the social values, values of Ubuntu sharing, are still very strong."[65] Ubuntu is the African philosophy of humaneness and caring for others, also expressed by the phrase "People are people through other people."

Still, there is evidence to suggest that despite the good news for young people such as Ciko Thomas, affirmative action has yet to make a significant dent in an economy where, according to the BusinessMap Foundation, fewer than 30 of the 450 companies listed on the Johannesburg stock exchange have significant black ownership.

South African economist Sampie Terreblanche worries that the low levels of education of many Africans have made them ineligible for employment in the service sector, which has grown significantly since 1960. He noted that some 2.5 million young people have entered the labor market but been unable to attain permanent jobs, increasing the unemployment rate. "In 2001," Terreblanche wrote in his book *A History of Inequality in South Africa*, "about 50 percent of African entrants to the job market could not find jobs in the formal sector. This lack of employment is a major reason for the poverty of 60 percent of the black population. This situation of structural unemployment and poverty has a compulsory character, because it is beyond the control of the unemployed. Although they are no longer systematically exploited, the poorer 50 percent of the population are still systematically excluded from most of the privileges of the new system of democratic capitalism."[66]

This situation holds the potential for serious social disruption. One of the biggest ticking time bombs in the country is the legions of unemployed youth, with little education and virtually no skills. Will they remain as patient as their elders, who from time to time express frustration but remain loyal to the ruling ANC? Even successful young entrepreneurs such as Ciko Thomas see the storm clouds on the horizon. "I think it's gonna take the society a long time," he said, "and we're gonna go through a lot of pain. And I always say, I just pray that it happens quick enough that you don't have social unease."[67]

A little over a decade into its new democracy, South Africa is in some ways where America was in 1968, when the country's inner cities erupted in flames sparked by rage. Back then, President Johnson's Kerner Commission reached a conclusion that took most Americans by surprise: America was in fact two societies, one white and prospering, one black and in decline. While there are no signs yet of such an explosion in South Africa, there are worries about poverty, still holding at some 45 percent, and unemployment, which was over 26 percent in 2005.[68]

Despite these gloomy figures, the post-apartheid government has made great strides, building more than 1.6 million new houses and providing electricity and water to millions for the first time (albeit, by the government's own admission, that is far less than what is needed). White alienation and resentment are on the decline; some thirty thousand whites who took millions of dollars—and themselves—out of the country over a decade ago, as the prospect of a black-led government loomed, have since applied to bring themselves and their funds back, their South Africanness winning out over their fears. And would-be domestic terrorists have been apprehended and put on trial, such as members of a right-wing group calling itself the Boermag, intent on returning South Africa to white rule. They set off bombs in the black township of Soweto, killing a mother of three, and placing bombs in several other locations. Experts such as Professor Albert Venter of the former Rand Afrikaans University (now the University of Johannesburg) say that such extremist groups represent the views of perhaps 5 to 6 percent of South Africans, but most predict that support for any kind of violent uprising or acts is even less.

Crime in general remains a key challenge for the black-led government. The violence of the apartheid years has left deep scars in the psyches and souls of many South Africans, black and white, and this often gets played out in violent behavior that makes dramatic headlines at home and abroad, fueling the perception of South Africa as an unusually violent place. Sometimes dubbed "the murder capital of the world," South Africa does in fact have has some of the highest rates of violent crime anywhere. But the murder rate has been dropping consistently since 1994, decreasing from 66.9 per 100,000 population then to 42 per 100,000 in 2004. And, contrary to popular perceptions outside of the country, the "new news" is that most murders are committed by people known to each other, with much of that confined to poor black areas where apartheid's brutality took its greatest toll.

Much of what is fueling the high murder rate is "intimate femicide," or domestic violence—the murder of a woman by her partner. According to a study by the Medical Research Council, the University of Cape Town, and the Centre for the Study of Violence and Reconciliation, a woman is killed by her partner every six hours in South Africa—"the highest that has ever been reported in research anywhere in the world." The perpetrators are most likely to be blue-collar, farm, or security workers.[69]

"Glaring income disparities, high unemployment, easy access to illegal firearms and alcohol abuse have all been linked by analysts to South Africa's rates of violent crime," as Reuters reported.[70]

One of the most emotionally difficult stories I've ever had to report was the rape of a five-month-old girl whose mother had left her in a tiny makeshift room behind the projection room of an old movie house. When I saw the child, she was lying still in a hospital bed, her large, dark eyes alert to every voice and movement, her face a silent testament to the pain she had endured. The young attending physician could barely contain her own anguish as she described the baby's injuries, ripped as she had been from her vagina to her anus. I decided not to rehearse, but instead to speak from the heart of a woman rather than the head of a journalist. I remember saying how hard it was for me to look at this innocent creature and imagine how anyone could have done such a thing to her.

Over the next few days I brought several other mothers, friends of mine, to see her in the hope that one might be moved to take her from this place. One did, and the child has had warm and loving care ever since. In the long court proceedings prior to her adoption by my friend, the child's mother appeared, disheveled and clearly suffering from too many desperate, sordid nights in the streets.

There is a widespread belief that the rape of children, particularly infants, is related to the myth that sex with a virgin or an infant will prevent or cure AIDS. Though a number of analysts believe that some men may have in fact been influenced by such a myth, most argue that the facts belie such an idea. Rape of children predates the AIDS pandemic and, according to extensive studies of the problem, is part of a cycle of abuse; "no single idea can be held to be the culprit."[71]

Like everywhere else in the world, the media reporting in South Africa follow the time-worn dictum "If it bleeds, it leads," leading to a disproportionate amount of sensationalist headlines about the most bizarre or daring crimes, and that adds to the perception of South Africa as a violent place. Even in affluent, predominantly white neighborhoods of Johannesburg, where there is relatively little crime, the high walls built around houses during the apartheid days remain, as the fear of invasion remains. In my own moderate-to-upscale neighborhood in Johannesburg, I noticed renovations going on at a recently purchased house. The first thing the new owners did was build a new wall, several feet taller than the very tall one that previously existed. But there are no such walls in the still squalid black townships, where the majority of black people live and where most of the crime is committed.

In 1994, the new majority South African government inherited not one but eleven police forces, many coming from the "black homelands" created by the apartheid regime to keep the races separate. "Some [police forces] didn't have minimum requirements [for candidates] other than health, and a large number were illiterate," recalled Gareth Newham, project manager for crime and police at the Centre for the Study of Violence and Reconciliation. But, according to Newham, there has been "drastic improvement," with new applicants required to have a high school diploma, a driver's license, and no criminal record. "The caliber [of police officer] is much higher," he said, and as a result, the police are having a "better impact."[72]

Early into South Africa's new nonracial democracy, criminal syndicates began organizing, taking advantage of a temporary vacuum as the new majority government replaced the old white regime. Most of the more dangerous crime, such as armed robbery and carjacking, can be traced to these syndicates. But in recent years those crimes have decreased as organized crime task forces have targeted the syndicates. More than 250 crime organizations have been cracked in the past few years, according to Newham.

Moreover, Newham indicated, a more studied approach to South Africa's crime identified 145 of the 1,100 police precincts in the county as areas where most of the crime was concentrated. They tended to be in the inner city and townships. As a result, authorities concentrated on bolstering community-sector policing, creating smaller sectors where police could get to know the community, facilitating communication and problem solving.

Police corruption remains a major challenge, with few results since it became a national priority in 1996, according to analysts. But by 2004, a majority of South Africans claimed to be satisfied with policing, for the first time since the black-led government came to power, Newham noted. Improved social and political conditions, including wider access to education, have been big factors in crime reduction.

South Africa is unique. Since it shed the shackles and sanctions of apartheid, the country is no longer "the polecat of the world," as Nelson Mandela once put it. Quite the contrary—it is fast becoming the brightest jewel on the African continent, busy establishing itself as the continental superpower. South African business—long kept homebound by the country's racist politics—is now eagerly making up for lost time, spreading its wings into the rest of the continent, selling other African countries everything from mobile phones to hydroelectric plants, with many of these ventures led by black-owned or -managed companies.

Moreover, despite the lingering negative perceptions, mostly in the West, of the country's current president, Thabo Mbeki, stemming from his confusing position on AIDS, Mbeki is arguably the most visible, most outspoken, and most effective leader presently on the continent. He had nurtured the idea of an African renaissance at least as far back as his early days in exile in the seventies, but the platform from which he sounded it in the nineties, as Nelson Mandela's deputy president, made his message resonate. As he told members of South Africa's National Assembly in June 1997:

> Gradually and perhaps in infinitesimal ways, we are, as a people, making such contribution as we are capable of making towards the creation of a better universe.
>
> The success of our common project to remake South Africa as a stable, non-racial, non-sexist and prosperous democracy depends in good measure on the coterminous existence of an international community, similarly defined.
>
> Among other things, this places on us the obligation to contribute to the common African continental effort, at last to achieve an African Renaissance, including the estab-

lishment of stable democracies, respect for human rights, an end to violent conflicts and a better life for all the peoples of Africa.[73]

Mbeki has spearheaded efforts to bring about this renaissance, logging tens of thousands of miles at home and abroad to spread his neo-pan-Africanist mantra: Africans must take control of their own destiny, sort out their own problems, and create their own solutions. They must come to the developed world not with a begging bowl but with offers of partnership, with the focus on remedying problems, many of which the developed world helped create.

Mbeki secured a second five-year term as president in 2004 when his African National Congress racked up 70 percent of the vote. He took that as a mandate to pursue his vision, with South Africa's future inextricably tied to that of the rest of the continent around and above it. He paid little attention to criticisms, again from mostly white-dominated parties, that he spent too much time solving other countries' problems at the expense of his own country's, or—the other side of that coin—that he paid too little attention, or at least the wrong kind, to Zimbabwe, South Africa's troublesome neighbor to the north. Mbeki seemed less concerned with the daily criticism than with his historical legacy, although from time to time through *ANC Today*, his unique, must-read online weekly newsletter, he engaged in lengthy debates—sometimes bordering on the picayune—with critics ranging from Archbishop Desmond Tutu to those who are less prominent but no less vocal, such as Charlene Smith, a former journalist who became an AIDS activist after being raped in 1999 (though she has remained HIV-negative).

Whatever his faults, Mbeki has brought to his own country and to the continent a renewed sense of their possibilities and their Africanness. "I am an African," he declared from the parliamentary podium in 1996 on the adoption of the two-year-old multiracial democracy's constitution, when he was still Nelson Mandela's deputy president.

> I owe my being to the hills and the valleys, the mountains and the glades, the rivers, the deserts, the trees, the flowers, the seas and the ever-changing seasons that define the face of our native land. My body has frozen in our frosts and in our latter-day snows. It has thawed in the warmth of our sunshine and melted in the heat of the midday sun.
>
> The crack and the rumble of the summer thunders, lashed by startling lightning, have been a cause both of trembling and of hope.[74]

A duality echoes in the souls and psyches of many South Africans, including the Thabo Mbeki I met in the eighties, while he was still in exile, quietly meeting white South African intellectuals and key actors on the apartheid stage, showing them a radically different side to their "*swart gevaar*" perceptions—many called him "charming" and "disarming." And yet he wrote to me once that he felt "like a cosmic wanderer, driven by the winds to land where they will. Every day it becomes more necessary to design a system to make a rational interpretation, to build a logical and systematic construct out of the myriad of actions and activities which I explain as contributions to the general effort to end the apartheid system."[75]

George D'eath (pronounced "dey-ahth") was one of the South African members of our reporting team working on "Apartheid's People." He had been an enormous help to me in decoding the details of apartheid, and he had gone with me day after tension-filled day as we ducked and dodged agents of the apartheid state. In the evenings, as we unwound in the smoke-filled haunts of musicians and artists and other free spirits in

Hillbrow, then one of the few areas blacks and whites could go without being hassled by the authorities, George would agonize about his future. (Today Hillbrow is a teeming slum playing host to thousands of mostly illegal immigrants from as far away as Lagos and Addis Ababa, and a venue of ongoing criminality and police raids that only seem to deter, not defeat. But in 1985 it was a cool place to be.) George loved his country, and he hated apartheid. As my U.S.-based team was leaving, he gave me a book, David Lamb's *The Africans*. In the book George wrote a little note calling my attention to the last lines of the introduction, saying he hoped they would come to be "the first lines for a better future for us Africans": "But, troubled as these early years of nationhood have been, Africa need not dwell forever in the uncertain twilight zone. Its dreams have been only mislaid, not lost."[76]

Not long after that, George traveled to New York, and he and I had a great romp down Broadway, where I took him to buy something he could wear to a going-away party for one of his American friends. He remarked about how he wished for the day that we, a black woman and a white man, could do that in Johannesburg, as unremarked by passersby as we were that day in Manhattan. A year later, he was dead, hacked to death with machetes while filming township violence, caught between government-backed black groups and anti-apartheid activists.

Today as I sit in Rosebank and watch the mixed couples sipping cappuccinos, some attending their cappuccino-colored babies and laughing with abandon, I often think of George and wonder what he would make of how his country's search for that "mislaid" dream has turned out. We might discuss the unmet needs of millions of Africans still living in shacks, those without access to running water or electricity, especially in the rural areas, where access to health care remains difficult and where land reform is painfully slow, but we might also discuss the results of a 2005 survey that found 93 percent of the country's citizens are proud to be South African.[77]

On a daily basis, South Africans from all walks of life are showing a positive commitment to making their country work. The democracy established in 1994, with the most liberal constitution in the world, has led to a free and open society, with all the necessary statutes in place to ensure the fulfillment of its promise. Political debates may be heated, but they no longer take place in an environment as poisonous as that of the early nineties, when the political violence led to the deaths of thousands.

Still, young democracies, like older ones, are tested on a daily basis. And South Africa is not unique in that regard. One of its biggest tests—not only of its young democracy but of its president—commenced on June 14, 2005, when Mbeki fired the country's deputy president, Jacob Zuma, in what Mbeki said was "the interest of the Honorable Deputy President, the government, our young democratic system and our country."[78] The action followed the conviction and sentencing of the deputy president's business advisor, Shabir Shaik, arising from charges of fraud and corruption. The case revolved around Shaik's soliciting a bribe on behalf of the deputy president from a French company bidding on a multibillion-dollar government arms contract. Based on this and other financial dealings, including Shaik's writing off some $154,000 worth of Zuma's unpaid debts, Justice Hillary Squires concluded in his ruling that Shaik had a generally corrupt relationship with the deputy president.[79]

While vocal supporters burned T-shirts bearing President Mbeki's image and staged spirited demonstrations against him in the deputy president's home province of KwaZulu-Natal, research revealed that at least 63 percent of the nation supported the president, with some 62 percent of blacks in his corner. The president's national approval rating reached at all-time high of

65 percent, even as it declined in KwaZulu-Natal. "This is a concerning finding," noted the marketing research company Research Surveys, "as it represents a philosophy that rejects the judiciary particularly in one province, KwaZulu-Natal."[80]

Former deputy president Zuma was subsequently charged with two counts of corruption, but vowed to fight to clear his name. "I have not committed any crime against the state or the people of South Africa," he said in his June 14 statement of resignation. "All said and done, I believe that we should put national unity and the interests of our country and nation first— whatever views people may have about the President's decision and the Durban Court judgment."[81] But Zuma did not remove himself from his position as deputy president of the ruling African National Congress, which puts him in line to succeed Mbeki when the latter concludes his second five-year term as president of the country in 2009.

As tensions rose and the environment became increasingly polarized, a Sunday newspaper reported that Zuma was being investigated on charges he had raped a woman who had been an overnight guest in his home, a charge he denied.[82] This not only added fuel to the fire but served as a reminder of the political innuendo and poisonous dirty tricks used in the past. It added to widespread concerns about how this would affect the standing South Africa has achieved internationally as a proponent and practitioner of good governance.

Zuma's corruption trial was scheduled to begin in July 2006, and whatever the outcome, it may signal the end of innocence for South Africa's young democracy, with the verdict having far-reaching consequences for the powers of the presidency.

When I first came to South Africa in 1985, I was offended by Afrikaners' description of South Africa as both "first world and third world." It seemed to me that they were trying to justify apartheid by saying that blacks weren't equipped or ready for a modern society, and so they would have to remain in their subservience until such time as they came up to "white standards."

Not even the most diehard Afrikaner would make that claim today, many being more concerned about diminishing opportunities for them and other whites in the society. Earlier, Mbeki talked about "two societies"—but not in the same way Afrikaners had described it. Mbeki's was a distinction that looked at the poor black majority and the prosperous white minority. But by 2005, he was talking of "two economies"—a broader, more inclusive description that takes into account all of those left out, but still with an emphasis on the long-excluded black poor.[83]

South Africa is still in the early stages of its new democracy, with its own unique challenges, but with many of the same growing pains experienced in the United States in the early years of its democracy. In those days, a black individual was defined in the U.S. Constitution as three-fifths of a person. It took time and blood to change that, and it took even more time and more blood to secure the full rights guaranteed in the amended Constitution, to which my own history bears witness.

Thus, it is through the prism of the United States' history that I daily bear witness to the changes occurring in South Africa, and that is the yardstick by which I measure its progress. I am not agnostic on South Africa getting it right. I want to believe with Martin Luther King Jr. that "the arc of the universe is long, but it bends toward justice."[84]

In 1994 South Africa took a giant leap on its path to justice, but so long as the country's income disparities are among the highest in the world, the country's victory is incomplete. That has been acknowledged by its young ruling party, which continues to tinker with its social and economic policies. But if South

Africa succeeds in bringing about an economic revolution that shifts control of the economy from the white minority to the black majority, it will be one of the most profound developments in the history of the continent, if not the world. And that will hold out the prospect of reviving an entire continent and ushering in the African renaissance.

So, what is Africa to me?

In South Africa, it is the movement of the most powerful black-led country in the world toward its own renaissance, with all its fits and starts, offering me a once-in-a-lifetime opportunity to observe and report its "new news."

# chapter TWO

# Baby Steps to Democracy

*I*t should come as no surprise that Africa is a continent on the move, especially if one is familiar with the phrase *"ex Africa semper aliquid novi"*—something new always comes out of Africa. But for those who feed on a steady diet of bad news about the continent, the fact that there is some new news out of Africa might indeed come as a surprise.

In 1960 British prime minister Harold Macmillan spoke of the "wind of change" blowing through the continent as its countries began breaking free of the chains of colonialism.[1] But there is a second wind blowing through the continent today: the forty-eight countries of sub-Saharan Africa are attempting to break free of the lingering legacy of colonialism, as well as many of the demons of their own design. This second wind holds out the promise of some of the most dramatic developments since Africans christened the new nation of Ghana as "the turning point of the continent," as described by Kwame Nkrumah in 1957.

Ghana's independence opened the door to a stampede of independent nations, and to the hope and expectation that Africa, the birthplace of humankind, would regain the glory it lost over the decades of colonialist exploitation, slavery, and degradation. Or, as Congolese poet and prime minister Patrice Lumumba wrote:

> The banks of a great river in flower with hope
> Are yours from this time onward.
> The earth and all its riches
> Are yours from this time onward.[2]

But the turning point Nkrumah spoke of led, in time, to a dead end for Africa. On the "banks of a great river in flower with hope" lay not only the dead body of Lumumba, the victim of Western-assisted assassination and misguided African ambition, but the detritus of broken promises and misrule, conflicts in and among nations, tens of millions dead or suffering, and hope, "like truth, crushed to earth."[3]

For too long a litany of sad songs has dominated the story of Africa and fueled a relentless, unforgiving Afro-pessimism. But the new news comes from hope, like truth, rising from the earth as Africans take steps to realize an African renaissance, becoming masters of their own fate, charting their own way out of the four D's of the African apocalypse—death, disease, disaster, and despair—which have made the continent the sorrow child of the universe.

Africans are now seeing differently, with grand ideas, arising out of a grand vision created and shared by progressive (and some not-so-progressive) leaders on the continent. It was conceived by five African presidents: South Africa's Thabo Mbeki, Algeria's Abdelaziz Bouteflika, Egypt's Hosni Mubarak, Nigeria's Olusegun Obasanjo, and Senegal's Abdoulaye Wade. And though its name is not as elegant as its vision, the instrument of this vision nevertheless has a name: the New Partnership for African Development, widely known as NEPAD (pronounced *neh-pad*). Its goal is to eliminate poverty, concentrating on growth and development, halting marginalization of Africa in the global arena, and accelerating the empowerment of women.

But while Africans want to run their own show, they realize that with few exceptions, most countries on the continent are too poor to go it alone. Therefore, they set up a bargain with the West: Africans get control of their political and economic houses in exchange for help with resources to build adequate housing and create jobs that will erase the reality of one in two Africans—some 315 million people—living on under $1 a day, implement programs that will help stem the spread of AIDS, distribute medicines to treat or eliminate diseases such as malaria and tuberculosis, provide food that will feed the legions of the hungry, and make available education that will feed Africans' minds and, in time, help Africans to feed themselves.[4]

NEPAD also hopes to change overwhelmingly negative perceptions of Africa as a continent buckling under the weight of disease, disaster, death, and despair, as well as corruption. To be sure, the four D's—plus one C—have been major factors in retarding Africa's progress, along with such natural disasters as drought and floods. These phenomena have provided the backdrop to most coverage of Africa, determining the way Africa is perceived, especially in the West. Such perceptions have been a major factor in discouraging much-needed foreign investment, but they have also become self-fulfilling prophecies, sometimes nipping incentive in the bud. International agencies have come to the rescue with food and other kinds of aid in many countries, but their generosity, while life-saving in numerous instances, has also led to a dependency that in some cases has removed the incentive for, if not the desire of, Africans to provide for themselves.

NEPAD was born as the African Union (AU), a new continent-wide organization, was finding its sea legs. The African Union took the place of the Organization of African

Unity (OAU), a body founded in Addis Ababa, Ethiopia, in
1963, with the primary focus on eradicating all forms of colonialism. With that mission long since accomplished, in 2002 the
OAU transformed itself into a new organization with a new
mission and new marching orders, with its first chairperson,
South Africa's president, Thabo Mbeki, outlining the goals in
themes he had long championed:

> By forming the Union, the peoples of our continent have
> made the unequivocal statement that Africa must unite!
> We as Africans have a common and a shared destiny.
> Together, we must redefine this destiny for a better life for
> all the people of this continent.
>
> The first task is to achieve unity, solidarity, cohesion,
> cooperation among peoples of Africa and African states. We
> must build all the institutions necessary to deepen polit-
> ical, economic and social integration of the African con-
> tinent. We must deepen the culture of collective action in
> Africa and in our relations with the rest of the world.[5]

Mbeki went on to talk about the need for developing partnerships with all segments of society and heralding a new and more
proactive role for the AU.

> As Africans, we have come to understand that there can
> be no sustainable development without peace, without
> security and without stability. The Constitutive Act pro-
> vides mechanisms to address this change which stands
> between the people of Africa and their ability and capacity
> to defeat poverty, disease and ignorance.
>
> Together we must work for peace, security, and stability
> for the people of this continent. We must end the senseless
> conflicts and wars on our continent which have caused so
> much pain and suffering to our people and turned many of

them into refugees and displaced and forced others into exile.[6]

These pronouncements made for some of the most dramatic new news to date. African sovereignty had been one of the pillars of the Organization of African Unity, with borders sacrosanct. As a result, critics often referred to it as "a dictators' club." Now, in a dramatic break with tradition, Mbeki was sending the message that the new African Union was not going to let leaders do wrong—steal, countenance corruption, commit human rights abuses, or fight among themselves or with their neighbors —and then hide behind sovereignty, hindering continental development.

To that end, the AU agreed on the African Peer Review Mechanism—a voluntary process that would allow member states to submit to a review of their political governance as a part of the deal for Western investment and aid. Western nations have indicated a willingness to help but have made it clear that the most support will go to those countries that get the best reviews. As of January 2006, twenty-six of the fifty-three African states that are members of the AU (Morocco is the sole state on the continent that did not choose membership) had signed up to participate in the self-monitoring program, although only two, Ghana and Rwanda, had actually gone through the full process.

South Africa's Thabo Mbeki, whose term as AU chair ended after one year, led mediation and conflict resolution in some of the most intractable cases on the continent, the success of South Africa's own inclusive, negotiated settlement providing the framework for his approach.

For more than forty-five days in early 2003, South Africa hosted alienated parties to a conflict that held the prospect of igniting a continent-wide war. The war in the Democratic

Republic of the Congo, in the heart of the continent, lasted four years, with massive collateral damage—the deaths from malaria, dysentery, or violence of up to three million people, mostly innocent civilians scattered across a country of fifty-five million that is the size of all of Western Europe.

Mbeki invited the warring parties to South Africa's lavish Sun City Resort, about a two-hour drive from Johannesburg. During apartheid, Sun City was located in what was then called a homeland, one of several mini-states created by the white minority regime to keep the black majority ethnically segregated and white South Africa autonomous and intact. Sun City was infamous for hosting black/white liaisons, usually white South African men having illicit rendezvous with black women. But since the end of apartheid, the resort has become a popular tourist attraction, complete with world-class golf courses and casinos, and it is a short ride from game parks featuring leopards, lions, rhinos, Cape buffalos, and elephants.

The Congolese participants, many of whom came straight to Sun City from long periods of fighting in the often harsh conditions in the African bush, were housed in lovely rooms on the expansive, lush grounds, fed, and entertained, all on South Africa's tab. When the talks went past forty-five days, South Africa put its foot down: reach a deal by the weekend or go home. It worked, give or take a day.

According to some estimates, the bill came to over U.S. $3 million. But clearly Mbeki and his team believed this was a small price to pay to secure a peace agreement that he saw as a giant step toward the realization of the African renaissance he had nurtured since his exile days in the seventies and which he has repeatedly called for since he assumed office, first articulating it publicly in 1996. The energetic leader was a constant presence, along with his team of experts, often participating in talks into the wee hours of the morning.

"The South African experience was appealing to most of the Congolese," remembered Professor Ernest Wamba dia Wamba, one of the participants. "No Congolese party was totally opposed to Mbeki, especially given the conditions of work put at their disposal."[7]

Largely through dogged determination, South Africa was able to announce a peace deal that resulted in an interim power-sharing government in the Congo and a promise to cease hostilities. The plan called for holding elections within two years, giving voice to a devastated people who had had no say in their own destiny since independence from Belgium more than forty years previously. Few familiar with the chaotic conditions of the country believed elections would happen in that time frame, but most thought they would eventually take place.

This development, though long and hard in coming, was new news after Congo's long night of bad news, dating back generations—and which was aided and abetted by the United States and its "national interests." For decades, the United States propped up an autocratic dictator, the late Mobutu Sese Seko (born Joseph-Désiré Mobutu), allowing him to get away with gross violations of human rights and corruption, so long as he served the interests of the United States as a bulwark against Soviet Communism during the Cold War. Mobutu amassed a fortune while his people got poorer and poorer in their diamond- and mineral-rich nation, and the United States looked the other way.

In the mid-1950s Mobutu aligned himself with the nationalist movement that ultimately ousted Belgium, the country's pernicious colonial ruler. But Mobutu was later associated with the murder of the popular nationalist government leader Patrice Lumumba, and in 1965 Mobutu took power in a coup d'état, elevating himself to president in 1970. Mobutu then launched a program of "national authenticity," changing the country's

name to Zaire and his own to Mobutu Sese Seko Kuku
Ngbendu wa za Banga—"the all-powerful warrior who, because
of his endurance and inflexible will to win, will go from conquest to conquest leaving fire in his wake."

But for all that, Mobutu will be remembered not for his
"national authenticity" but for "national kleptocracy." He
became rich by dipping into state-owned enterprises and sharing with family, friends, generals, and others he needed to keep
in line. "Mobutu and his entourage helped themselves to state
revenue so freely that the Congolese government ceased to
function," wrote Adam Hochschild in his acclaimed history of
the Congo.[8] By some estimates, at one point Mobutu was worth
some $4 billion.

Mobutu also ruled with an iron fist, murdering opponents
and ruthlessly stifling dissent, ironically even recalling the
troops from Belgium to help suppress rebellions. But Mobutu's
political fortunes declined with his health. The United States
had no more use for him after the Cold War ended, and used his
corruption and human rights abuses as a reason for cutting off
aid. Mobutu, meanwhile, had developed prostate cancer, and
as his country slid further into decline, the ailing autocrat paid
less and less attention to national affairs, dying eventually in
Morocco in 1997, a few months after being overthrown by
Laurent Kabila.

Kabila, who steamrolled to power with the help of neighboring Uganda, Rwanda, and Angola, proved to be no more of a
statesman during the three and a half years he was in power. He
was assassinated in January 2001, and his twenty-nine-year-old
son, Joseph, a major general in the army, was installed as president. While it is too early to tell how he will fare on history's
report card, young Kabila committed himself to the South
Africa-brokered peace deal, including a new constitution and
democratic elections. But the Congo remains a messy, fragile

place, with militias fighting among themselves in the eastern part of the country, displacing some 100,000 people and threatening lasting peace in the country.

Still, some of the new news is that Mobutu's death signaled the beginning of the end of the era of the African "big man," and perhaps the first best chance to fundamentally change the rules they established and bent at their whim. Not all of the old big men have died, but they are dying or otherwise fading from the scene. And many of the guns of war have also been silenced, primarily by Africans inserting themselves in the affairs of sovereign states, against all past pattern and practice.

In Burundi, where more than a decade of ethnic conflict between Hutus and Tutsis has left a death toll of more than 300,000, a fragile peace, brokered initially by former South African president Nelson Mandela in 2001, led ultimately to a power-sharing government and a provisional constitution, put in place in 2004. Pierre Nkurunziza, a former rebel leader, was elected president in August 2005, the "first president chosen through democratic means since the start of Burundi's civil war."[9]

The belligerence hasn't died out altogether, but Mbeki and a team of South Africans have remained engaged. The relative success of such missions led shortly thereafter to Mbeki being tapped by the African Union to attempt mediation in a crisis that had reached civil war proportions in Côte d'Ivoire, a former French colony in West Africa.

Côte d'Ivoire also had its "big man"—a somewhat more benign one—for thirty-three years following independence. Breaking ranks with the preponderance of state-run economies of the day, Félix Houphouët-Boigny embraced the free market and encouraged foreign investment, setting his country on a course of relative prosperity over the decades after independence in 1960. The country became one of the world's largest exporters of cocoa, though it also generated income from the export of coffee beans and palm oil.

But Houphouët's death in 1993 marked the beginning of a decade-long downward spiral of violence and civil war, dividing the country along religious lines—a predominantly Christian south and a predominantly Muslim north. The spark for the violence stemmed from the government's refusal to allow Alassane Ouattara to stand as a candidate in the presidential poll of 2000 after a coup in December 1999. Though Ouattara had served as Houphouët's prime minister from 1990 to 1993, the government under coup leader Robert Guei ruled that Ouattara could not be a candidate because he was not an Ivorian citizen, which required that both parents be Ivorian, and Ouattara's mother was said to have been from neighboring Burkina Faso (though Ouattara disputed this). But this new demand for "Ivoirité," or Ivorianness, ultimately led to the 2002 failed coup attempt against the eventual winner of that poll, Laurent Gbagbo, and the subsequent civil war.

The troubles in Côte d'Ivoire led to foreign investment drying up. The situation deteriorated further in November 2004, when Gbagbo's troops attacked French peacekeeping forces, killing nine. A frantic, hastily organized mass exodus followed, especially of French residents, along with a UN arms embargo.

The French, who over the years had maintained close relations with their former colony, including ongoing investments, initially took swipes at Mbeki's involvement, insisting the South African didn't understand the nuances of Ivorian politics, despite the fact that France's own peace accord negotiated in January 2003 fell apart.[10]

Undeterred, Mbeki flew to Côte d'Ivoire on more than one occasion, receiving a rousing reception in the otherwise tense city of Abidjan. Mbeki also summoned all of the parties involved in the conflict, together and/or separately, to South Africa for several rounds of talks.

His tireless mediation paid off in early April 2005, when the parties agreed to cease hostilities and begin working toward new elections in October. The final sticking point—Ouattara's ability to run for president—was removed when a few days later Gbagbo agreed to allow him to be a candidate.

Gbagbo lauded Mbeki's leadership in the context of the "African solutions for African problems" paradigm. "We have had a lot of mediators before and people would impose on us solutions to our problem," he said, adding that Mbeki had mediated "with clarity and humility." Even the French praised the outcome of Mbeki's mediation. And while few, if any, believed these developments heralded an end to the country's problems, even Ouattara talked the talk, calling the decision to allow him to run "an incontestable first step toward democracy in Côte d'Ivoire."[11]

African leaders such as Mbeki and Nigeria's Olusegun Obasanjo are hoping to add Côte d'Ivoire to a string of democratic successes around the continent that would provide incontrovertible proof of Africa's new path, despite intransigence on the part of the warring parties that delayed elections scheduled in that country for October 2005. Obasanjo brought to bear not only the weight of the African Union, which he chaired at the time, but the winds of democratic change that had been blowing through his own country. Nowhere were the hopes higher than in the continent's most populous country, Nigeria, home to almost 130 million people, the largest population on the continent.[12] Obasanjo is one of the architects of NEPAD, and his country a key test of it and the continent-wide effort to help make the twenty-first century the "African century."

Obasanjo, a former military ruler, was widely applauded for the rare move of handing over power in a voluntary transition to civilian rule in 1979. His criticism of subsequent military regimes, including that of the murderous and corrupt military dictator Sani Abacha, earned him international respect—and also landed him in prison for three years. He was later released and ran successfully for president as a civilian candidate. In 2003 he ran for a second term in the first civilian-run election in twenty years. More than 24 million Nigerians voted.

A successful outcome to the Nigerian elections was important not just as a test of NEPAD but also given Nigeria's status as the one of the largest producers of oil in the world. This has taken on added significance for the United States, which began looking for alternatives to Middle Eastern oil after 9/11.

Despite the country's vast oil resources, most Nigerians live in poverty, with two-thirds of its people living on less than $1 a day, according to the World Bank. One factor in this discrepancy is corruption. The Berlin-based NGO Transparency International, which monitors corruption worldwide, ranks Nigeria as the third most corrupt country in the world, after Bangladesh and Haiti.[13]

But under Obasanjo the country declared war on corruption, and the president insisted that his administration was "fully poised to deal ruthlessly with corruption in all its ramifications." The government has "ruffled some highly placed feathers for alleged corruption charges," according to the newspaper *This Day*, including a former education minister, a former president of the senate, and a former minister of housing.[14] Even so, the reckoning has been slow in coming. By late 2005, only one prominent figure had been sent to jail, but that was nevertheless historic. The former inspector-general of police, Tafa Balogun, was imprisoned for six months for corruptly enriching himself to the tune of nearly 15 billion naira (more than $100 million US).

Nigeria has been plagued by violence in both the north and south of the country. In the north, Islamic law is in force, meting out harsh punishments, including death by stoning of women for having sex outside marriage. In 2002, the Miss World pageant pulled out of Nigeria after a newspaper article led to a violent upheaval between Christians and Muslims, resulting in 200 dead, 1,200 wounded, and 12,000 homeless. The offending passage of the article had asked whether or not Muhammad, the paramount prophet of Islam, would have wanted to marry one of the contestants if he had been alive.

Meanwhile, in the oil-rich delta in the south, there had been continuing violence over efforts by the local population to gain an equitable share of the region's oil wealth. Violence stemming from one issue or another has led to the deaths of some 10,000 Nigerians in various parts of the country since 1999, including Ken Saro-Wiwa, the prize-winning author and activist, who in 1995 was hanged along with eight Ogonis for speaking out against the exploitation of his people. Not even a plea from Nelson Mandela, then the world-respected leader of South Africa, could save him.

Against this backdrop, there were concerns about Nigeria's election in 2003. Like the vast country itself, the election that brought Obasanjo back to power was robust and raucous, the loser in the presidential contest calling it "a massive and state-organized rape of democracy."[15] Some international observers also found fault with the process.[16]

But Chris Fomunyoh, who led a team from the National Democratic Institute for International Affairs, based in Washington, said even against the backdrop of such irregularities, there was hope in the fact that many of those who felt cheated were following the legal processes set up for their grievances:

That by itself is really a step forward and a reconfirmation—a confirmation of the fact that democracy is beginning to take root. So hopefully by the time this all blows itself out, we may see a Nigeria that is stronger and better

prepared to embrace or continue to move along the democratic path in a way that could be beneficial to Nigerians
but also to the African continent, because we must keep in
mind that one of every seven Africans is Nigerian—that
Nigeria is playing a very powerful role, or seeking to play a
very powerful role within the African Union, and Nigeria
with an Obasanjo that's viewed as legitimate, a government that is viewed as legitimate, and having been elected
through the democratic means, stands a better chance of
being able to provide that leadership than would be the
case if its credibility or its democratic credentials were
questionable.[17]

Obasanjo's renaissance partner, Thabo Mbeki, along with
former South African president Nelson Mandela and Don
McKinnon, the secretary-general of the thirty-four-member
Commonwealth of Nations, joined other notables in prais-
ing the "success" of Nigeria's elections, with Mbeki agreeing
with African Union observers, led by Senegalese politician
Abdoulaye Bathily, that "any aggrieved party should fully utilise
the existing legal mechanisms to deal with any matters of
dispute."[18]

Obasanjo invited comments about "the details of observed
shortcomings [so as] to enable corrections and the right lessons
to be learnt for future use," adding: "No human activity can be
regarded as perfect because perfection can only be found with
God."[19] Grumbling and griping, but no coup d'état. And while
Nigeria still faced enormous challenges, ranging from the continuing violence and corruption to the economic hardships of
most of its people, Africa's most populous country contributed
its share of new news out of Africa.

At the same time, old habits die hard, as events in Togo in early
2005 demonstrated. Togo, a former French colony, is a tiny West

African country of some five million people. Early in 2005, the president, Gnassingbé Eyadéma, the continent's longest-ruling dictator, died of a heart attack. The iron-fisted ruler had held the top office for more than thirty-eight years.

Shortly after his death, the military installed his son, Faure Gnassingbé, as head of state. Demonstrators took to the streets, demanding elections. At the same time, the fifteen-member Economic Community of West African States (ECOWAS) threatened the country with sanctions unless it returned to constitutional order. The African Union condemned the events, which it called a coup. And Nigeria's Obasanjo, as head of the African Union, called for elections.

After days of unrest and violence, Gnassingbé bowed to internal and external pressure and agreed to step down until an election could be organized. Prior to the election, Nigeria's Obasanjo summoned Gnassingbé and opposition leader Gilchrist Olympio to Abuja, the Nigerian capital, and brokered a deal that would involve the creation of a government of national reconciliation, a move supported by the United States and the African Union. Olympio, a political exile who used an ally, Bob Akitani, as his stand-in for the election, thanked Obasanjo, saying Togo had much to learn from democratic countries: "You have all said that there have been many years in the wilderness. Now there is a small opening that we wish to exploit. We call it transition, because we are going through a difficult period that will usher in democratic rule, the rule of law and respect for human rights." And Obasanjo underscored that the two leaders had agreed that there would be "an examination of the constitution to fashion out an amendment in order to satisfy the ideal of democracy and fundamental human rights."[20]

But following Gnassingbé's win with 1,325,622 votes, or 60 percent of the total cast, the losing candidate, Bob Akitani, condemned the vote as fraudulent and issued a call for Togo's youth to fight the government. The call was answered: as the Associated Press reported, "mobs of young men raged across the capital of Lomé, setting stacks of tires ablaze and unleashing plumes of smoke that darkened the horizon. Through the afternoon, security forces with tear gas and concussion grenades scattered the protestors."[21] At least three died, and many were injured.

Thus tiny Togo loomed large as a test of NEPAD's goal of good governance and democratic practice. The jury will be out for a while on young Gnassingbé, but the hope is that African leaders will not allow a younger generation of "big men" to take the place of their fathers, whether biological or spiritual. Meanwhile, Togo should not be allowed to disappear from international focus, for whatever happens there will help determine how seriously the promise of African solutions to African problems should be taken.

Meanwhile, an even stronger challenger to the principles of NEPAD could be found on the other side of the continent in Zimbabwe, a country with democratic institutions but undemocratic behavior. The elections of 2002 and 2005 were hailed as "free and fair" by an assortment of African organizations but were roundly criticized by the United States, the European Union, and a few African analysts as seriously flawed. But Zimbabwe's troubles with the international community didn't start there. They were preceded by President Robert Mugabe's controversial and often violent land reform program.

The issue of land redistribution to black Zimbabweans is long-standing and complex. But the basic fact is that for generations a small minority of whites owned the majority of Zimbabwe's arable land, while the majority of blacks remained landless and poor. No one denies that the land issue had been simmering for some time and needed to be addressed. But many have taken issue with the way in which the Mugabe government proceeded, starting with its backing in 2000 of a band of angry war veterans who began seizing white-owned farms and became increasingly violent. While distancing itself from the violence, the government called the invasions a matter of redressing the imbalance of land allocation that had developed over the years.

The massive land seizures occurred against the backdrop of the government's first electoral defeat since independence, when voters overwhelmingly rejected an amendment to the constitution that would have given the government powers to seize land without compensation, as well as extend the president's term of office, making Mugabe eligible to serve up to thirty years.

At the same time, a feisty young labor-based opposition party, the Movement for Democratic Change, had recently emerged. It consisted of many of the disenchanted white farmers and young black urban voters born after the struggle for independence and therefore with few, if any, emotional ties to the ruling party and those who waged the struggle. The fact that Mugabe was a freedom fighter who led the country to independence in 1980 is ancient history to many of them. Their activism helped defeat the referendum and led to the government's ongoing denunciation of the MDC as a tool of white interests. But it also served as a wake-up call for the ruling ZANU-PF party, causing it to mobilize the instruments of the state and terrorize members of the opposition as well as its supporters. Among the government's new arsenal was a youth brigade known as the Green Bombers. Its members tortured, raped, and killed government opponents with the blessing of the government, some of the former Green Bombers told me after they had fled to South Africa. I also interviewed MDC members who showed me the burn marks on their bodies from torture with electric shock. Later, I spoke with doctors who confirmed they had treated these and other opposition supporters who had been tortured. One young man who claimed to be a former Green Bomber told me he personally had killed five people and that he had been trained "how to kill a person not making noise . . . having a piece of cloth so you can close his mouth, then breaking his neck."[22] The Mugabe government consistently denied wrongdoing by the Green Bombers, arguing that the sites many said were devoted to terror training were in fact camps aimed at promoting good citizenship among the youth.

In 2000, Zimbabweans went to the polls in a parliamentary election that saw the MDC capture 57 of the body's 120 seats—not enough to block the ruling party from forming a new government, but enough to block any constitutional change. That was a second wake-up call for the increasingly beleaguered government.

In 2002, as violence escalated—most of which was attributed by observers to government supporters and officials—almost three million voters nevertheless turned out to vote in the presidential poll. The election was chaotic, with voters attempting to cast their ballots but often finding no record of their registration. A one-day extension of the voting period was granted, but a second, called for by the opposition, was denied. Thousands, many of whom had slept on the ground overnight, were left in seemingly endless lines without a chance to cast their ballots. Most of these lived in urban areas—the strongholds of the opposition MDC.

During a crowded postelection press conference, the Commonwealth observer group, led by former Nigerian military ruler Abdulsalami Abubakar, pointed to the high levels of violence and intimidation before and during the election, citing mostly supporters of the ruling ZANU-PF party. He capped off his report with these words: "All the foregoing conditions in Zimbabwe did not adequately allow for a free expression of will during the elections." Subsequently, citing election rigging and persecution of dissidents, the Commonwealth suspended Zimbabwe's membership in the group (Zimbabwe withdrew a year later).[23]

The victorious ZANU-PF ruling party denounced the Commonwealth findings. The opposition MDC called for new elections and launched a court challenge to the results. But the MDC was severely crippled when the government brought charges of treason against its leader, Morgan Tsvangirai. And while he was eventually acquitted, the trial lasted some two years, and during that time the possibility of a death sentence from a court many believed in the pocket of the government hung over his head. The whole process took much of the steam out of the MDC's efforts to position themselves as an alternative to the ruling ZANU-PF party.

The MDC initially wavered on the issue of taking part in the parliamentary elections of 2005 but finally agreed to participate, despite the absence of a resolution to their earlier election challenge. Moreover, the organization's ability to conduct its campaign was constrained by a series of laws the government had enacted in the interim. The Public Order and Security Act (POSA) of 2002 required government permission for any assembly of more than five people, leading to the harassment and arrest of many opposition leaders and supporters.[24]

In contrast to the 2002 presidential election, the 2005 parliamentary elections went off with few hitches and few lines outside polling places. Gone also were the overt violence and palpable climate of fear that had characterized the 2002 election. But a climate of fear still prevailed, with the government still holding all the security trump cards through the arsenal of laws it now had on the books, POSA in particular.

For example, Section 12 of POSA makes it a criminal offense to do or say anything that may cause "disaffection" among the police or defense forces, punishable by a fine and/or imprisonment of up to two years. Section 15, among other things, makes it an offense punishable by a fine and/or up to five years in prison to publish statements that incite or promote public disorder or public violence, adversely affect the defense or economic interests of the country, undermine public confidence in the police, prison service, or defense forces, or interfere with any essential service. Section 16 makes it an offense to insult the president. Sections 17 and 19 allow for the imprisonment of up to ten years of individuals who disturb the peace or say or do anything that is considered obscene or insulting. And Sections 23–31 regulate the organization and conduct of public gatherings and provide the police with extensive powers to control them, including the requirement that police be given four days' advance notice for holding public gatherings or meetings.

Amnesty International, among other human rights organizations, condemned these provisions, arguing the police "actively used these provisions to strictly police peaceful meetings and have, to some degree, made Zimbabwe a police state where democratic activity is tightly controlled and supervised, and where repression of internationally recognized human rights is the commonplace."[25] Moreover, Amnesty International and others argued that the government used the POSA provisions "to specifically target the MDC and hamper their ability to campaign and mobilize support, particularly in the run-up to elections."[26]

The Zimbabwe government insisted that laws such as POSA are necessary to deal with threats to public safety. Prior to the 2005 election, the government also proposed legislation aimed at limiting the activities of nongovernmental organizations, including voter education.

Meanwhile, political developments in Zimbabwe have not taken place in a vacuum. The country of more than 12 million had a promising start as an independent nation in 1980, investing in education and raising the country's literacy level to one of the highest on the continent. But in the subsequent quarter century Zimbabwe has gone from being the breadbasket of Africa to an African basket case. Recurring drought caused some of the country's problems, but economic mismanagement and corruption have been critical factors, leading to skyrocketing inflation and a drop in GDP of more than 30 percent between 2002 and 2005.[27] Inflation went as high as 623 percent in 2004, and while it dipped somewhat in early 2005, by October of that year it was back up to 411 percent, "buoyed mainly by soaring prices for bicycles as chronic fuel shortages forced more people to give up driving."[28]

At the same time, the country had nearly run out of maize meal, the nation's staple, along with other basics such as cooking oil, sugar, and margarine. The prices continued to rise on what little food there was, putting it out of reach of the average Zimbabwean, as unemployment stood at around 70 percent.[29]

"Even optimistic growth projections for a post-Mugabe Zimbabwe suggest it will take 15 to 20 years to regain the living standards of the mid-90's because of the breakdown of the country's economic backbone—agriculture," concluded Dianna Games in her pre-election report of 2005.[30]

In early 2005, the U.S. Agency for International Development's FewsNet reported: "Staple foods and their primary substitutes continue to be available at most urban and rural markets in varying quantities throughout the marketing year. However, employment opportunities remain bleak. The formal sector last year lost more jobs than it created."[31]

After insisting prior to the election that there was ample food in the country, the Zimbabwean government later announced it was making plans to import food. Meanwhile, critics accused the government of hoarding food prior to the election and using it as a weapon to reward its supporters and punish opposition supporters. Most food security analysts predicted that access to food would be a continuing problem for the poor.

Much of the country's food scarcity and other problems are the result of the government's land reform program, which led to external sanctions and further deterioration of the economy. The violence that accompanied the land grabs led to an exodus of white farmers and the collapse of the commercial farming sector, with tens of thousands of black Zimbabweans thrown out of work and subsequently having to rely on being fed by international aid agencies.

In one of my visits to the country in 2003, I witnessed lines of up to eleven thousand people in one feeding location, where half-starved mothers carrying unsmiling babies with dull eyes joined others after hours-long treks to get the rations of maize and cooking oil that they said would last them, at best, two weeks. After that, they would have to get by on whatever they could scratch out of the dry, parched land. Down the road from the feeding center, I stopped to talk with a farmer who was waiting for his wife's return from the center. He took me to his field of young green corn that had no chance of maturing due to the drought, which has claimed his crop for three seasons in a row. When I asked him how he got by once the food aid ran out, he reached down into the tall grass and pulled up a handful.

"We boil this," he said plaintively. "This is how we survive."

Still, as Peta Thornycraft, one of Zimbabwe's most fearless journalists, reported: "Mugabe said [in 2004] that donors should divert resources to other countries as Zimbabweans would 'choke' if any more food aid was delivered."[32]

A steady decline in donor funding due to what Western agencies regarded as bad governance has, according to UNICEF, contributed to a steady deterioration in the health of Zimbabweans of all ages. UNICEF figures show that the mortality rate for children under five has risen 50 percent since 1990, translating into one death for every eight births; one hundred babies become HIV-positive every day; one in five Zimbabwean children is now an orphan (the majority from AIDS); a child dies every fifteen minutes from HIV/AIDS; and 160,000 children will experience the death of a parent in 2005.[33]

South Africa's Thabo Mbeki has had little of the success in Zimbabwe that he has enjoyed elsewhere, having embarked on a strategy of "constructive engagement" and made many attempts to resolve the political stalemate. He traveled to the country on several occasions and met with both sides. But by mid-2005, despite his assurances that a solution was imminent, not only was there no sign of any rapprochement between the opposition and the ruling party, but the opposition MDC indicated in no uncertain terms that it had lost faith in South Africa's ability to act as an honest broker, given its endorsement of the 2005 election as credible. Moreover, in May 2005 the entire African group formed a consensus supporting Zimbabwe's reelection to the UN Commission on Human Rights, opening still another divide between North and South as Australia, the United States, and Canada strongly protested.

There have been no signs of movement toward a more open society in Zimbabwe. If anything, the government became even more repressive following its election victory in 2005. Shortly after the elections, the government launched "Operation Drive Out Rubbish," which it claimed was aimed at putting black marketeers out of business, removing street traders, and shutting down illegal vendors, all of which the government claimed were undermining the economy. But critics questioned why the sweep was taking place only in areas where the government had lost to the opposition in the two previous elections. The United Nations special envoy, Anna Kajumalo Tibaijuka, reported that the evictions had "precipitated a humanitarian crisis of immense proportions," and said the operation "rendered over half a million people . . . either homeless or living with friends and relatives in overcrowded and health threatening conditions."[34] The envoy called on the government to halt the mass evictions, charging they violated international law. Amnesty International condemned the evictions. One evicted grandmother asked a nun who was trying to help: "Why has God abandoned us?"

The nun, Sister Patricia Walsh of the Dominican Missionary Sisters, wrote that when she arrived at one of the sites where the sweep had taken place, "I wept, Sister Carina was with me, she wept, the people tried to console us—they were ALL outside in the midst of their broken houses, furniture and goods all over the place, children screaming, sick people in agony. Some of the people who are on ARV drugs [antiretroviral drug therapy for AIDS treatment] came to us and said, '[W]e are phoning Sister Gaudiosa (Sister is doing the ARV programme) but she is not answering us, we are going to die.' We explained that Sister was on home leave but that we would help in whatever way we could. It was a heartbreaking situation."[35]

The Roman Catholic archbishop of Bulawayo, Pius Ncube, has consistently used his church as a bully pulpit, speaking out against human rights abuse and condemning in the strongest terms the 2005 election. Women's groups such as Women of Zimbabwe Arise (WOZA) staged prayer vigils and marches for justice, even in the face of arrests and beatings by police. And other civil society organizations such as the Crisis Coalition, made up of more than 350 civic groups, continued to challenge what they saw as unjust laws and government repression long after the polls had closed and the election was decided. The government might have won the election, but it did not win the hearts and minds of those who believe it didn't play fair or who are concerned about its capacity to rescue the country from further deterioration and international isolation.

As with Togo, the growing willingness of people to stand up and speak out and demand that their government respect the principles now being espoused all over the continent under NEPAD, at great cost to themselves, is inspired by the second wind blowing across the continent. And that is part of the new news. Meanwhile, with the trend toward democratic elections, however flawed, the question has arisen as to whether this means the end of the tendency for opposition groups to cry foul after elections or, worse, stage coups. Chris Fomunyoh noted:

> The fact [is] that countries such as Senegal and Benin and Mali and Ghana have gone through credible elections that have brought about a change of power through the ballot box; . . . there is some hope that Africa's future does exist and that the younger generation of Africans, even if it inherits a continent that's got substantial problems, is going to be able to make a contribution to make the continent much better.[36]

But the question remains: just how many "committed democrats" are there on the continent? When the new African Union was launched in 2002, replacing the thirty-nine-year-old Organization of African Unity, one of the notable naysayers was Libyan leader Muammar Ghadaffi, who expressed skepticism, if not contempt, about its prescription for Western aid, calling it a potential tool for "blackmail and exploitation."

I met Libya's inscrutable leader in July 2002 in the large tent he had had flown in to Durban, South Africa, in which he entertained other heads of state and guests attending the African Union launch. He told me in my exclusive interview that the majority of African leaders—most of whom, like him, do not lead democratic governments—agreed with him. "If the assistance or if the terms of assistance are coupled and conditioned with political aspects, like the governance or the democracy or human rights, then this is considered to be an insult and will not be accepted."[37] Ghadaffi has yet to sign up for the peer review or to hold elections in his country.

But democratic progress can be measured in more than elections, and for this, by way of example, I return to South Africa.

During a Millennium Review I did of the continent's democratic progress, as the United States was still debating the results of the 2000 presidential election and its problems in Florida in particular, South Africa's foreign minister told me: "We've seen one of the older democracies in the U.S., when all fails in the 'country of votes or dimples' . . . this or the other institutions had to come in and resolve the impasse. So it's important to have democratic institutions that support the democratic processes."[38] To that end, South Africa took two covert slush funds it had discovered from the apartheid era and used them to strengthen emerging democracies. Moreover, it donated resources and space for the permanent home of the Pan-African Parliament, a new continent-wide body whose key objectives include promoting the principles of human rights and democracy in Africa, and increasing pressure on those member states who continue to fall afoul of the democratic standards implicit in the African Union's Constitutive Act, the Africa Charter on Human and People's Rights, and the AU's Declaration on the Principles Governing Democratic Elections in Africa.[39] It is also designed to serve as a forum for parliamentarians across Africa to debate issues and give ordinary Africans a voice in developing their continent.

The body, with 202 legislators from forty-one of the fifty-three member states of the African Union, has advisory powers only, but is expected eventually to have full legislative powers. In a sign of the emergence of women in politics, the president of the Pan-African Parliament is Gertrude Mongela, from Tanzania.

Early on, many wondered if the Pan-African Parliament might not become just another African "talk shop." That remains to be seen. But the urgency for it and other institutions aimed at strengthening democracy on the continent is driven not only by a need to convince the West but also by the need to convince Africans themselves of what's being called the "democracy dividend." Clearly, as the Togolese and Zimbabwean cases suggest, there is growing support among ordinary citizens for democracy on the continent, with people willing to put their bodies on the line to achieve it.

At the same time, NEPAD is not without its critics, including one of its own architects, Senegal's president, Abdoulaye Wade, who in 2004 complained that the project has been too slow in delivering. In response, Wiseman Nkuhlu, a South African who is the chair of the NEPAD Steering Committee, has emphasized that NEPAD itself does not initiate projects and that its goals are long-term, not expected to bear fruit before some twenty to forty years have elapsed. But can NEPAD sustain interest and garner support at home and abroad without immediate, tangible examples of its utility? How can it maintain the momentum needed for the long haul without some dividends?

These issues arise at a moment when the African Union's own survival is an open question, given that it has not overcome the problem of keeping itself financially afloat. The AU's budget for its Addis Ababa–based staff, including ten commissioners, was a mere $43 million in 2004, with projections that the organization's needs are almost four times that. Many analysts agree with Prince Mashele, a senior researcher at the Pretoria-based Institute for Security Studies, that "it is very doubtful they will get the money."[40]

Most African countries are deeply in debt to Western institutions and insist they don't have money to pay either dues or special assessments.[41] This severely limits the capacity of the organization, especially to meet the growing demands for African peacekeepers, particularly in high-conflict areas such as the Darfur region of Sudan, where the United States and others have concluded a genocide is occurring against the African tribal farmers in the region. More than two million have been terrorized by the Janjaweed, a government-backed militia on a campaign of murdering, raping, and branding young girls and women, killing men and boys, and destroying villagers' food and water supplies. It was widely reported that the goal of the Janjaweed was to wipe out the indigenous African inhabitants, who the Khartoum-based government insisted provided a base for two rebel movements opposing the government.

Haunted by the international community's failure to prevent the genocide in Rwanda in 1994, many called for U.S. support of the beleaguered African Union, including former UN ambassador Richard Holbrooke and U.S. senator Jon Corzine, who both visited Darfur in 2004. "The United States and NATO should offer airlift and logistical support to the impoverished African Union to aid its monitoring mission—and that mission, with strong UN Security Council support, should evolve rapidly into a full-fledged peace-keeping operation," Holbrook and Corzine said, also calling for the appointment of a U.S. ambassador to the African Union.[42]

Among the other daunting challenges for the AU is Somalia, where more than fifteen years of anarchic conflict have prevented a government elected in exile from returning to reestablish democracy. Violent warlords have balked at having foreign troops on Somali soil, but the country's exiled leadership has reiterated its determination to bring in an AU force of peacekeepers. But again, the problem of resources may prove more of an obstacle than objections on the ground. "The AU is more effective when it comes to politics, less effective when it comes to implementation of its decisions," said the Institute for Security Studies' Mashale.[43]

It is clear that there are severe constraints on the capacity of Africans to provide comprehensive solutions to African problems, especially when it comes to the all-important role of peacekeeping. While African nations—especially Nigeria and South Africa—have committed troops to peacekeeping missions around the continent, most of Africa's countries cannot afford more than a token contribution to peacekeeping or enforcement missions. Here the need for partnerships with the West is critical, especially for training and logistical support, if not for troops on the ground.

On another front, many called for more inclusiveness in the NEPAD process, saying that it had been too "top-down." South Africa hosted two conferences aimed at fostering more participation from the grassroots, and in 2005 the AU created the Economic, Cultural and Social Council to facilitate more cross-fertilization between the leadership and those they lead.

Meanwhile, some who supported the concept of "African solutions to African problems" now argue that the time has come to revisit that concept. It became a refrain after the 1994 Rwanda genocide, during which the international community stood by while more than 800,000 Tutsis and moderate Hutus were massacred by Hutu extremists. But the National Democratic Institute's Christopher Fomunyoh argues that the phrase has now "lost its rationale" and that the "outdated and obsolete dictum" has been

misused by autocratic regimes in countries such as Zimbabwe, Sudan, Togo, Guinea and Cameroon, who claim that the rest of the world has no business criticizing their human rights violations, stolen elections and culture of corruption. On the other hand, the slogan provides

solace to some bureaucrats in donor countries who are
reluctant or unwilling to propose bold steps that can bring
their countries to assist Africa in its path. Even "friends of
Africa" are left wondering whether their genuine efforts
and initiatives would be second-guessed ad n[a]useum or
met with excessive hostility and unnecessary criticism by
those they intend to assist.[44]

John Stremlau, former head of the Department of International
Relations at the University of the Witwatersrand in Johannesburg, voiced other reasons for concern about the slogan, which
he said could be used as "a cop-out for the rest of the world doing
nothing." But Stremlau is against jettisoning the phrase. Rather,
he argues that Africans need the same kind of help, encouragement, and cooperation the United States gave to Europe via the
Marshall Plan as that continent rebuilt after the Second World
War.[45] In fact, in 2005, Britain's prime minister, Tony Blair, in
launching the Commission on Africa, which included several
African heads of state and top government officials, called for a
something like a Marshall Plan for Africa and for wealthy countries to double aid to Africa. He has called Africa the "scar on the
conscience of the world" and commented that the impoverish-
ment of Africa presented "the fundamental moral challenge of
our time."[46] The new news is that one of the leading industrial
nations stepped up to put Africa and its needs prominently on
the agenda of the Western world.

  While Blair lined up pledges from a number of European
Union members to double overall aid for Africa over the next
ten years, the plan failed to win the endorsement of the United
States, which opposed a key element: an International Finance
Facility (IFF), whereby the richest nations would guarantee
long-term but conditional funding to the poorest nations,
increasing the total amount of aid provided by the rich countries

by $10 billion a year over a decade, with the goal being $100 billion per year by 2015. The Bush administration cited the U.S. "legislative process" as its reason for opposing the plan, insisting it could not limit the freedom of action of a future Congress. Other reasons cited included Congress's unwillingness to support the idea and concerns over potential misuse of the funds.[47] The administration also noted that U.S. aid to Africa "has almost tripled" during its tenure in the White House. But Steven Radelet, a senior fellow at the Center for Global Development in Washington, told the *New York Times* that American aid to Africa, totaling less than $5 a year per African, is "about the same as what many Americans spend each morning for coffee and a bran muffin."[48] Most Americans believe the United States spends 24 percent of its budget on poor countries, but the actual figure is less than one-quarter of 1 percent. This stands in contrast to Blair's call for the wealthy nations to increase aid to 0.7 percent of national income.[49]

During a trip to Washington in early June, a month prior to the G-8 summit in Gleneagles, Scotland, Blair lobbied the U.S. president to support his plan. But before the G-8 meeting, Bush launched a preemptive strike, promising to double U.S. aid to Africa over the next five years and proposing a $1.2 billion program to combat malaria in Africa through 2008, $400 million for an Africa Education Initiative, and $55 million "to promote women's justice and empowerment in four African nations." The president also announced the release of $674 million in humanitarian aid that had been allocated by Congress earlier. Much of the funds would go to famine-stricken Ethiopia and Eritrea. But critics such as Africa Action's Salih Booker argued that what Africa needs most is not food aid but development assistance, which ultimately might render food aid unnecessary.[50]

In 2000 the United Nations set a goal of cutting poverty in half by 2015. This is a tall order for Africa in particular. Since

1981, the number of Africans in extreme poverty—living on less than a dollar a day—has doubled, to some 315 million.[51]

But Africans (and their supporters outside the continent) are generally united around the proposition that the best international instrument for helping to reduce the continent's poverty is debt cancellation. The continent's aggregate debt is somewhere between U.S. $250 billion and $300 billion, with Africa's external debt per capita, at $365, exceeding GNP per capita, which is $308. In 1996 sub-Saharan Africa, minus South Africa, paid some $2.5 billion more in debt servicing than it received in new long-term loans and credits.[52] Thus the prayer of Aden Abdullahi, a member of the East African Legislative Assembly: "If God can forgive us of our sins, I cannot understand why we cannot be forgiven our debts."[53]

There is widespread agreement that there is plenty of blame to go around on this draining indebtedness, which has its roots in the 1970s and 1980s, when Western lenders rewarded despotic regimes that supported U.S. "national interests," determined more often than not by Cold War calculations. The mistakes were made by both borrowers and lenders, explained Salih Booker, as "much of the money went into the hands of unrepresentative and repressive governments."

Booker went on, "There is a concept called 'odious debt.' That's when loans were made to a repressive tyrant and the money was not used for the intended purposes. So when the tyrant goes, the debt should go. Otherwise, you have people paying for their own repression."[54]

Moreover, aid from agencies such as the International Monetary Fund and the World Bank came with burdensome conditions that required massive cuts in social spending, including education and health care, with devastating effects on the poor.

However, despite pledges from Western nations as far back as 1999 to assist in writing off $100 billion of debt owed by poor countries, under the World Bank and International Monetary Fund's Heavily Indebted Poor Countries Initiative, Africa's debt remains staggering.[55]

A growing chorus of both governmental and nongovernmental voices, ranging from Nelson Mandela to rock star Bono, have called for urgent action on debt relief. In mid-2005 movement began toward 100 percent debt cancellation for fourteen African countries. This was hailed by some as "an important first step," in the words of Shadrack Gutto, of the University of South Africa's Centre for African Renaissance Studies, but he, like most African analysts and advocates of debt relief, has argued it is far from enough. The G-8 nations, he and others insist, have a long way to go toward fully meeting their obligations to Africa's poor nations.[56]

Clearly, there is still a bumpy road ahead. But for the first time in some forty years, Africans at all levels of society are looking at taking their lives into their own hands. And while they may debate, sometimes vociferously, what are the best strategies to transform their societies and their continent, the new news is that there is something substantive to these debates, and the debates are, as it were, taking place within the family. NEPAD may not be perfect, but its potential for perfection rests with the collaboration of African leaders, businesspeople, intellectuals, students, and ordinary people now coming together in a way that Africa has not seen since the mobilization to end colonialism and apartheid. "The seeds are being planted," as Shadrack Gutto put it, citing the "new and creative ways Africans have introduced to resolve conflicts."[57]

The examples come not just from South Africa's decade-plus of peace and stability, but from what up to now have been some of the most intractable and deadly conflicts. The Congo is now on the path to democracy, largely due to South Africa's mediation. In Sudan, agreements have committed the former combatants to working together to achieve peace and stability In Liberia, a new day may be dawning with the historic election of Africa's first woman president, Ellen Johnson Sirleaf, in November 2005. Her election followed a period of relative stability after Nigeria's Obasanjo orchestrated the removal of Charles Taylor, a ruthless leader who shattered his own country and destabilized the entire region during an almost two-decade-long civil war. Obasanjo gave Taylor asylum in Nigeria in 2003, over the objections of the United States, which has called for him to be tried in an international forum as a war criminal. But Obasanjo's action helped prevent still another genocide and helped set Liberia on a path to peace, stability, and democracy.

It is too early to say peace is breaking out on the continent, for there is still low-level fighting occurring even in countries that have signed peace agreements, as well as in dreadful cases such as Darfur, in Sudan, where by most accounts a genocide occurred with the blessing and support of the Sudanese government. But however small and tentative the steps toward democracy, some footprints can be seen on the continent's vast landscape.

"Africa is creating for itself a time of opportunity the like of which we have not seen for a generation," said UN General Assembly president Jan Eliasson at the opening of the assembly in October 2005. "In 1998, 14 African countries were in a state of armed conflict or civil strive. Now the number engaged in major conflict is down to three."[58]

Moreover, no leader on the continent is standing up publicly and saying that democracy is not for Africa. As South African journalist Peter Fabricius wrote near the end of 2005: "As democracy gradually displaces dictatorship on the continent, fewer leaders are being removed from office feet first and more are going by peaceful processes."[59] Based on data from the Human Sciences Research Council of South Africa, Fabricius reports that between the independence of Ghana in 1960 and

2004, of 204 African leaders, 51 percent were removed from power by coup, war, or invasion; 2.9 percent were assassinated other than in a coup; 5.8 percent died of natural causes or accident; 12.2 percent retired voluntarily; 19.6 percent were impeached or removed by interim regimes, and just 7.8 percent were removed "in what is supposed to be the normal democratic manner, [i.e.,] they lost an election and left office." But, he added, the trend is positive. From 1960 to 1969, twenty-eight of the thirty-seven leaders who left office did so as the result of force; just one left voluntarily, and none did so after losing an election. By contrast, from 2000 to 2004, only four of the twenty-four leaders who left office were forced out by coup or war, and one was assassinated. Eight left office voluntarily, and three left after losing an election.[60]

What's more, the steps that are being taken to achieve the kinds of societies where governments are accountable to the people are a large part of what is providing new hope on the continent. From Togo to Zimbabwe and even South Africa, people are being blown by this second wind into the streets to demand rights, freedom, and justice. And while they may not yet see the light at the end of the tunnel, they have a road map and a realistic hope that in time they will get there.

Some examples: Even in Zimbabwe, where virtually all else has failed, in 2005 a soccer match between ordinary members of the ruling ZANU-PF party and the opposition Movement for Democratic Change was a step toward narrowing the divide. It was called "soccer diplomacy." Said Job Sikhala, an MDC parliamentarian who participated in the match, "We believe that the people of Zimbabwe need to go through a process of healing—these challenge soccer matches are a way of promoting peace and stability in the area. As residents and leaders in the community, we cannot sit back and watch people beating each other up."[61]

The most hopeful new news on the continent is that Africans have begun to set standards for the conduct and behavior of their leaders. By early 2006 twenty-six heads of state had signed a commitment to be judged on a regular basis by those standards, which will apply not just to the leader currently in power but to all who come after. And a group of former heads of state met in Bamako, Mali, in June of that year at the invitation of the National Democratic Institute and its African Statesmen Initiative. They pledged to help with peace and conflict resolution, to enter the fight against HIV/AIDS and other diseases, and to "use our good offices to foster dialogue and the peaceful resolution of the continent's conflicts, and to promote human security and democratic models of government that offer citizens the opportunity to choose their leaders freely and participate fully in the political life of their countries."[62] According to the NDI's Chris Fomunyoh, who organized the meeting, the former presidents were invited because they met three criteria: they had been democratically elected, they had lost an election and accepted the outcome, and they had committed themselves to contribute to good causes on the continent.[63] Twenty-three met the criteria. Fifteen showed up.

For those who report on and care about Africa's 800 million people, the newfound optimism within the continent is new news. The hope is that this optimism will spread beyond the continent, to those who owe it centuries-old debts, and that these countries will come forward and help Africans produce an Africa that will stand as a truly independent and full-fledged member of the family of nations.

# chapter Three

# Reporting
# Renaissance

*W*hen in 2000 *The Economist* devoted an entire issue to what it called "The Hopeless Continent," it fueled a widespread perception of Africa as a place of death, disaster, disease, and despair, the four D's of the African apocalypse—old news, as it were.[1] Indeed, *The Economist* was not alone in its negative portrayal of the continent, which is ongoing, especially in much of the international media. But the new wind blowing across the continent—a second wind, if you will—holds out the promise of an African renaissance, and with it a change in the way the continent is portrayed. Indeed, those in rebellion against the distortions of the past are generating "new news" on the continent, and many of them are African journalists.

"If there is to be an African renaissance, we, the media, remain a vital part of it," crusading Namibian editor Gwen Lister has said, joining a growing chorus of her continental colleagues from east to west and north to south.[2]

There have been dramatic changes in the journalistic climate on the continent within the last decade, with increasingly more independent media voices taking ownership of their own stories. Even journalists working for government-owned outlets are gaining new independence that enables them to do more than just regurgitate the party line, though that is still the case in far too many countries on the continent. But as more and more African leaders embrace the culture of democracy and its institutions, especially a free and unfettered press, journalists can more easily and more often speak truth to power.

A growing number of African leaders, like the journalists laboring among them, have come to understand the link between a free press and a free people and the advancement of their societies. And even where the government remains intransigent, the reemergence of the "guerrilla typewriters"—the underground reporting banned during the colonial and apartheid eras—is defying such repression, often at great personal risk to the journalists themselves. But those who undertake it are convinced that exposing the truth about corruption or abuse of power will be a positive contribution to widening the democratic space and to nation building.

The emergence of the African journalist also holds out the promise of influencing the perspective of international journalists, who all too often continue to feed the world distorted pictures of the continent. That is not to tar all foreign correspondents with that brush, as many have done stellar work and continue to do so, even when their editors back home show little enthusiasm for stories that go against the grain.

For example, international journalists sometimes have an advantage over local journalists, particularly when there is a thorny issue to be pursued. The foreigner can often get away with the tough questions because he or she doesn't live there and won't be affected in the long run by a resentful official.

Moreover, foreign journalists face barriers from some governments, which make access and accreditation difficult, if not impossible. This is especially true in countries that repress or control their own media. Thus, it is clear that there is enough ground to cover on the vast African continent for both domestic and foreign journalists, provided both are prepared to "come in right."

But the perception throughout Africa is that foreign media are only interested in stories that fit the old journalistic maxim "If it bleeds, it leads." Much of the shallow coverage of death, disaster, disease, and despair for which foreign media treatments of Africa are criticized derives from what is called "parachute journalism"—dropping in for a brief look at a situation, then flying back out without taking the time to delve deeply into the background or put a story in context. Judgments are often made in a vacuum, doing a disservice not only to the Africans but to the news consumers who need context, especially in the case of Africa, which is so poorly covered in general.

Many Africans have given up hope that the foreign media can ever be balanced in its coverage. But I believe international journalists can play a constructive role on the African continent, provided they "come in right."

"Coming in right" was affirmed for me when I was a young reporter covering Harlem in the late 1960s, as the space opened up by the American civil rights revolution was evolving into the Black Power movement, the slogan "Black is beautiful," and, for many of us, our first serious emotional contact with Africa. Many chose to go to the continent. The late Philippe Wamba, in his book *Kinship*, recalls the story of one African American who "greeted Africans at the Dakar harbor where he disembarked with an impassioned speech extolling the virtues of pan-Africanism and expressing his joy to be finally 'home.'" But the response he got was not what he had expected, Wamba reported. Instead, he heard: "Give us a dollar. You from America. You got plenty dollar. You be Big Man. America rich country. This be poor country. We need dollar. You give dollar."[3]

Not every African American who went to Africa had such an experience. And those who stayed at home were spared this reality check altogether, leaving us to make contact with the Motherland through, among other things, African names for many of us and our children. My own son's name, Chuma, comes from the Ibo of Nigeria and means "God's gift." Donning dashikis, wearing Afros, and reading intellectuals of the African diaspora such as Frantz Fanon provided our other contact.

In 1972, I was working for the *New York Times* and went to cover a press conference being held by the Black Panthers, who in those days were fighting against perceptions that they were a threat to national security, insisting instead on the debatable proposition that they were simply trying to uplift the community and take care of their own. When I arrived, a stern, intense young man wearing the Panthers' trademark black beret and matching black everything else asked what media organization I was from. As I once recounted the incident:

> When he learns that I work for the *Times*, he refuses. When I ask why, he says, "You work downtown for The Man, and The Man don't never have nothing good to say about Black People." He is surly and snide, but I persist. "But you don't know me or my work," I say. And he says, "But I know The Man ain't gonna let you print the truth." And I say, "I don't agree with that. What will it take to convince you to let me interview you?" And he says, "You got to 'come in right.'" So I say, "Let's make a deal. You let me interview you and then read the story in the paper tomorrow. If I don't 'come in right,' then you have the right never to talk to me ever again. Deal?" The young Panther ponders the offer, then says, "Deal, but I'm warning you."

I don't ask what he means by "come in right." I have covered Harlem long enough to know that its people, who are
constantly misrepresented in the press, don't want puff
pieces. They respect the truth and want the truth to be told
about them. I assume that "come in right" means honest,
fair reporting. The next time I see this young brother on
the street, he's read the story—and he's all smiles. "Right
on, Sistah," he says, giving me the clenched-fist Black
Power salute. I reply: "Power to the people."[4]

In the same article, I talked about Africans and their attitudes
toward American preconceptions about their continent:

One criticism I encounter from Africans is that Americans
present themselves to Africans as all-knowing, when, in
fact, their perspectives are influenced by the oft-distorted
views of Africa in textbooks and the media. In an attempt to
"come in right," I've tried to check my own views at the
door of the continent, realizing that I, too, am a product of
Western education and perspectives. Being an African
American, I have been propelled to go beyond traditional
sources, having experienced first-hand the sins of omis-
sion of those sources. In my own case, I believe being an
African American and a woman has been an asset, despite
the fact that African societies are still dominated by men—
and older, more tradition-bound ones at that. For me, it has
been a matter of understanding the culture, as I and African
women work in our own ways to change those things that
deprive us of our rights.[5]

Thus, when I set out for South Africa in the fall of 1997,
"coming in right" was one of the pieces of baggage I carried,
along with my trunks and suitcases. And that particular piece

of baggage has served me well, making me particularly sensitive to trying to strike a balance between stories of war, conflict, corruption, poverty, pestilence, and disease, on one hand, and, on the other, stories that tell us of the people who live amid all that and yet survive, endure, and sometimes prosper despite the odds. These people are the embodiment of new news, but they rarely, if ever, hold press conferences. As an old expression says, you have to go there to know there. And to know there and convey what you know to an audience outside Africa's borders is likely to lead to greater engagement with a continent whose people have not been given their fair share of the world's attention or resources, owed to Africa after centuries of colonial exploitation that carried over into the post-colonial world.

My point of entry into the continent was South Africa. From there, I would begin discovering the rest of the continent. But three years into its new multiracial democracy, even South Africa's "miracle" was losing its luster as a major story for Western media: all three U.S. networks had closed their bureaus, leaving only CNN. Apartheid had ended, and that, after all, was what had brought them there—the four D's all wrapped up in an overarching theme of good (the oppressed black majority) versus evil (the oppressive white minority).

But in my view, the story was just beginning. South Africa was emerging from being the "polecat of the world," as Nelson Mandela once termed it, and preparing to take its place as the superpower of the continent and a global citizen. It would take more than television's traditional minute-thirty to tell this story, one potentially as compelling as that of the fight to end colonialism, and one that would challenge the international media to "come in right."

My own approach to this potentially miraculous story was based on my three earlier assignments in South Africa during watershed moments in the country's evolution. In 1985, I had been assigned by PBS's *MacNeil/Lehrer NewsHour* to get beyond the predominant coverage of dramatic headlines and sound bites from a country in turmoil and present the story through its people in all their complexity. Here, as in the rest of the continent, I went after the stories that defied the clichés of Africa, hoping to bring to the audience I served the new news of Africa that nobody knew, taking viewers with me on a journey where together we would learn to see the things we had not previously been able to see.

My second reporting trip to South Africa came sooner than almost anybody could have imagined: 1990, when Nelson Mandela was released from prison after twenty-seven years. The moment was magical, even for the most hardened wag. My third assignment came in 1994, when I was to cover Mandela as he was about to become president of his country, and his long-banned African National Congress, the ruling party.

Each time I was in South Africa, the country was inundated with journalists from all over the world—in 1985 to cover the strife, and in 1990 and 1994 to report on the man who had gone from being seen by many in the West as a terrorist to being an icon all over the world. But for me, a major part of the excitement of the latter two assignments was in witnessing the peaceful transition of a society that could easily have erupted into civil war. To be sure, there was a great deal of violence in the run-up to the '94 election—most of it state-sponsored or state-supported. Thousands died, and yet many more would have if Mandela and the ANC had not agreed to a negotiated peace that left intact the predominantly Afrikaner civil service, the results of decades-long affirmative action in favor of whites. The ANC also agreed not to pursue any land claims dating back to before 1913.

The last big South Africa story for the international media was the Truth and Reconciliation Commission, which laid bare the still raw wounds of apartheid brutality and provided some of the most dramatic testimony ever of humankind's inhumanity to its own. For me, while it was a story focusing on the past, it was also laying the basis for new news, that is, a different kind of news— about how South Africa would survive the revelation of these horrible truths and what effect it would have on the reconciliation Nelson Mandela was espousing.

The hearings were at once painful for the victims, those who bore the tangible and intangible scars of apartheid's brutality, and for those of us covering the story, for some of the details touched the parts of us that were not protected by the wall of distance (some call it objectivity) we establish between ourselves and the people we write about.

A few months after I arrived in South Africa to cover stories on the continent for National Public Radio, I met some of the survivors who defied the clichés of Africa.

> Ida Radebe is one of them. I found her sitting on a chair in her small [d]ark house in the hills of a KwaZulu township. Her discomfort was visible as she extended her left leg, still swollen nine years after she was shot and left for dead during a funeral vigil in a neighbor's house. Eleven others died in a scene described by a policeman as so thick with blood that it covered their shoes and soaked their socks as they walked through the house conducting their investigation. Brian Mitchell, the white police captain who ordered the slaughter, served five and a half years in prison before being granted amnesty by South Africa's Truth Commission. After coming forward to tell the truth about what happened—a pre-condition of amnesty—Mitchell visited the KwaZulu community and asked for forgiveness. Not everyone forgave him, but despite the pain she felt even that day, Ida Radebe said: "I forgive Brian Mitchell with all my heart."[6]

A part of "coming in right" is understanding (and being able to convey) the context of a story—in this case, of South Africa's "miracle," not least because of its ongoing ramifications both inside and outside the country. Many of the journalists who crowded into hearing rooms around the country have long since departed, but the story is not over. There is new news in the efforts of those who suffered the sting of apartheid to find their justice and their peace, which they are not abandoning. At the same time, South Africa's process of reconciliation between former enemies, however imperfect, has become a model for conflict resolution on the continent and around the world.

It was indeed important to "come in right," as South Africa's new phase of its remarkable transition was just beginning—building a new, inclusive society out of an old one that had excluded its black majority. The story was especially compelling for me, given not only my reporting over the previous dozen years but also my longer historical perspective of having grown up in and triumphed over a system of injustice and oppression. The imperative that had driven my reporting since those early days was of unapologetically looking at things through the prism of my own experience, believing it served my journalism more honestly than any pretensions to an objectivity I don't subscribe to anyway.

I have been lucky to have worked alongside foreign journalists who work at "coming in right," and we learn from and lean on each other. And we often depend on local independent journalists to show us how to "come in right." Creating liaisons with African journalists on the ground has and will continue to go a long way toward defusing some of the charges against the foreign media. But that's not the point. The real point is to generate more accurate coverage of the continent and more realistic portrayals of its people. Moreover, by using the eyes and ears of local journalists, foreign reporters often get an angle on a story that wasn't obvious from the outside.

I remember being in Zimbabwe and attempting to get an update on the farm seizures. I had spent a morning with a white farmer who took me around, showing me the fields that lay fallow and the equipment that had fallen into disrepair because the invaders who had taken over the farms did not have the resources to get them fixed. But when I had finished that tour, a young Zimbabwean journalist I knew told me about how the government was now evicting the first wave of peasants it had used to seize the farms from the whites, removing them in order to give the farms to their politically connected cronies and re-latives. The journalist had covered the evictions as they were happening and took me to the area where they had occurred. The shacks the peasants had lived in had been burned to ensure that they would not return.

Much of the continent's attitude is that the foreign press, with its relentless focus on the negative, distorts the picture of Africa. Many have even called the coverage "racist." Such coverage has fueled what in recent years has come to be known as "Afro-pessimism"—the belief that there is no way out of the sinkhole that postcolonial Africa has become, which justifies wealthier countries' lack of involvement or investment. Ironically, it was an African American reporter who provided more ammunition to the Afro-pessimists when he declared that the Rwandan genocide had made him "thank God [that his] ancestor survived that voyage" that brought him as a slave to America.[7]

In the midst of Rwanda's genocide, it may indeed have been difficult to see beyond the blood, but even when we ourselves bleed, it is important for us to keep enough distance not to drown in it, reminding ourselves that we are witnesses to his-tory on behalf of a universe of people. The full record comes not from one account but from the totality of many different accounts appearing in many different places in many different formats.

What is important is that there be a record that helps provide the outline of lessons learned, so that, for example, the world will not be allowed to forget the consequences of doing nothing in Rwanda. More than 800,000 Tutsis and moderate Hutus are estimated to have been slaughtered in Rwanda in 1994 as the international community first ignored the situation, then dithered, delayed, and argued over the appropriate thing to call it and then what the appropriate response should be. The innocents who were massacred had not provoked it, and those they left behind cry out for a concerned world to know, appreciate, and act on their plight.

When I accompanied President Bill Clinton to Rwanda, on his first trip to Africa in 1998, I had already walked on the bloodied soil of the country, had seen the church where the clothes worn by dozens of men, women, and children murdered there remained strewn about amid the church benches, the skulls and bones of the dead removed to a small, otherwise unassuming shed of remembrance a few yards away. The horror of what I was seeing was almost too big to get my mind around—until my eyes fell on a tiny piece of ribbon that had once tied the hair of a child, stained by the blood of the one who had worn it.

I also met some of the children in Rwanda whose mothers and fathers were murdered in 1994. They had been forced into the role of head of household at ages as young as eleven. UNICEF estimated that there are 85,000 such households in Rwanda with more than 300,000 children living in them.

One of them was a fifteen-year-old with five younger brothers. As I described it in a magazine article:

For me, the story lay not so much in the tragedy of this young girl's life as in the heart beating inside her aching breast. A heart that revealed its strength when she was offered a few dollars by journalists who heard her story.

She listened in silence as they told her the money was hers to do with as she pleased. She took it, then disappeared inside the mud-and-wattle hut where she and her brothers lived. She aroused the youngest, who was about four and desperately ill with malaria, as evidenced by his distended stomach. She bathed him, then carried him to a road where she hitched a ride to a clinic miles away.[8]

Apologies would not fill their stomachs or treat the sick ones, but Bill Clinton, who had been president during the genocide and had not acted in time to stop the worst of it, felt the need to offer one on his visit. In a room packed with survivors, I wrote on my notepad Clinton's words:

The international community, together with nations in Africa, must bear its share of responsibility for this tragedy as well. We did not act quickly enough after the killing began. We should not have allowed the refugee camps to become safe havens for the killers. We did not immediately call these crimes by their rightful name: genocide. We cannot change the past. But we can and must do everything in our power to help you build a future without fear, and full of hope.[9]

And that hope is there—residing even in the souls of Africans from Rwanda and Darfur. Capturing that hope is essential to telling the African story, especially to those outside the borders of the continent. When foreigners are fed a steady diet of stories about hopelessness and despair, they are not persuaded to answer Bill Clinton's call. But when the continent and its people are portrayed accurately and consistently, not only will the rest of the world's people be better informed about a part of the world about which they have little knowledge, but they may also better appreciate how their leaders are responding and what they can do to help the innocent victims help themselves.

Today, Rwanda is rising from the ashes of its genocidal nightmare. The new news comes in part out of the efforts to deal with the Hutu militants who committed the genocide, known as *genocidaires*. Realizing that it would take generations for the overburdened Rwandan courts to try the more than 100,000 detained suspects, Rwanda instituted a system of gacaca adjudications, based on a traditional judicial process, that in some ways is similar to South Africa's Truth and Reconciliation Commission. Local people who have suffered through the terror have been trained to hear testimony and pass judgment. The process has its faults and critics, but it bears watching as a potentially groundbreaking experiment in conflict resolution and reconciliation. It is a part of the African story that is new news, even though it's incomplete.

Meanwhile, thousands of *genocidaires* belonging to the Interahamwe militia remain at large and committed to wiping out the Tutsi minority in Rwanda. Thus vigilance and engagement are still necessary—for Rwandans, for Africans, for the media, and for the international community.

It is also important to keep the spotlight on areas such as eastern Congo, where ethnic violence led to the massacre of close to a thousand men, women, and children. Likewise for Côte d'Ivoire, where in 2003 Ivorians used radio to stir up hatred against non-Ivorians, as Hutus had done in the 1994 Rwanda genocide. Côte d'Ivoire once had a vibrant, free press, but that institution has suffered during the political violence of recent years and has been downgraded by Freedom House to the status of "not free." This puts an additional responsibility on journalists outside the country both to make contact with the beleaguered journalists inside and to keep the country's story alive in their media.

Even as many of the continent's most devastating wars have
been brought to a close—in Congo, Angola, Sierra Leone,
Liberia, and Burundi, to name a few—the peace is ever so fragile, bearing close attention and scrutiny. Recalling the old/bad
news and putting it in context must also be a part of our new
news mission if there is to be any hope of the past instructing the
future. In the case of the Darfur genocide, this requires putting
the events in Sudan in the context of the world's failure on
Rwanda. Once again the UN was slow to call the systematic
slaughter of a people genocide, even after U.S. secretary of state
Colin Powell had done so. There was widespread condem-
nation of the actions of the Janjaweed, but the international
community did not put its full weight behind pressuring the
Sudanese government to stop the slaughter. Moreover, even
as Sudan remained on the list of state sponsors of international
terrorism, U.S. president George W. Bush forged a "close
intelligence partnership" with the Sudanese government and
failed to express moral outrage over Sudan's failure to stop
the slaughter. It is important for journalists—especially those
who communicate internationally—to keep such contradic-
tions before the public, which in free societies can use this information to hold their officials accountable and demand they
do the right thing. At a time when African leaders need all the
encouragement they can get to honor the principles of good
governance they themselves, have laid down, they also need
good global role models.

There are other stories on the continent that cry out for
attention as well—and which also call for balance, lest they
feed Afro-pessimism. Prominent among them is HIV/AIDS.
Sub-Saharan Africa is home to "more than 60% of all people
living with HIV—some 25.4 million," according to UNAIDS.[10]
The consequences of this pandemic will be felt for generations. As of mid-2005, the epidemic in countries such as South

Africa—which has the highest number of individuals living with HIV in a single nation—had yet to reach its peak, meaning that the death toll, even as it is causing cemeteries to run out of space, is going to go higher.[11]

For Africa's journalists, some of whom are themselves infected, the AIDS pandemic presents a peculiar challenge: striking a balance between nation-building journalism and the need to cover the stories that on the face of it convey still more bad news.

In general, African journalists have opted out of making AIDS a priority of their reporting. For example, in South Africa the media have been relentless critics of the government's approach to the pandemic, covering the court cases that resulted in policy changes such as making antiretroviral drug treatment more widely available to the poor. They also devoted considerable coverage to the aggressive advocacy of the Treatment Action Campaign, one of the most successful nongovernmental organizations to surface since the end of apartheid. But they backed off highlighting AIDS as a major issue during the 2004 presidential campaign. South African journalism professor Anton Harber told me he thought the media wanted to encourage the government in its slightly more energetic approach by suspending criticism for a while. At the same time, the media may have been following the lead of the South African public, which listed AIDS behind poverty and unemployment as the most important issues to them.

Some in the South African media, such as filmmaker/producer Xoliswa Sithole, have found the space (and the funds) to go deep into the AIDS story, reporting against the clichés. Sithole's documentary *Shouting Silent* grew out of her own pain and broke new ground in telling a story that had grown familiar. Sithole's mother died from complications of AIDS, which fueled her daughter's desire to look at the plight of other young women who have lost their mothers to the disease. She compassionately explored the interior lives of her subjects and the impact of AIDS on their families and their communities. Stigma and silence still surround the AIDS crisis, but work such as Sithole is contributing to helping end both.

AIDS is only one of many diseases threatening the lives and health of Africans, but it is in a class by itself in its impact. Although the saying "It takes a village to raise a child" came from Africa, the village is buckling under the weight of more than 11 million AIDS orphans, with more than 1 million in South Africa alone.[12]

Among other things, AIDS is assaulting the culture and traditions of the continent, slowly but surely causing the breakup of the extended family, the core of African life, as grandmothers and aunties and cousins are stretched beyond their limits, lacking the resources to take care of all the children left behind. In northern Namibia, a government health worker told me that the extended family is now so overburdened that people simply turn their heads during the mourning period when the discussion begins about what to do about the children of deceased parents. "So un-African," she told me. "But a sign of the times."

This is an important story to chronicle in all its devastating fury, and I offer no apologies for making it a priority of my reporting—that and the different ways, both good and bad, African governments are approaching the matter. For me, the way out of the clichéd reporting of the AIDS story is to focus on the people—those who suffer and die, but also those who live and hope. I wrote the story of Puseletso Takana, a winsome seventeen-year-old who had taken it upon herself to try to do something about the AIDS pandemic infecting half the girls her age in an impoverished village in the tiny mountain kingdom of Lesotho, where she lives. When I met her, she was writing and performing what she called "little dramas" aimed at educating her peers in the hopes of saving their lives. Stories such as hers are part of the new news of Africa's AIDS challenge and offer some small ray of hope amid otherwise relentless despair.

Once I was covering devastating floods in Mozambique that took the lives, homes, and possessions of so many of its people. I had found a family, the Mabasos, living in temporary shelter provided by a church after they had fled their waterlogged town some two hours away. The wife had been pregnant when the sudden rushing waters forced them to flee their home in the night. They made it out of the neighborhood onto higher ground, but the rising tide of water followed. They took shelter on the roof of a house. With the rains beating down, the wife went into labor, soon giving birth to first one baby girl, then another. It was three days before the rains slackened and the waters receded enough for them to climb down from the roof. By this time, one of the twins was dead. I turned to the father, who was a minister, and asked him what this awful time had done to his faith. To my amazement, he said it had made it stronger. "God could have taken all of my children," he explained. "Instead, He only took one."[13]

Faith like that is bound to take the edge off even the most cynical souls. Since I do not count myself among that group, what this man and his circumstances did for me was recalibrate my moral antennae and infuse my journalistic product with passion.

Stories of people who belie the stereotypes are not hard to find if journalists "come in right." For example, much of the world's perception of African music began with South African musicians who came in exile to America and brought with them the traditional mbaqanga rhythms of the townships. Miriam Makeba and Hugh Masekela opened this door, going back to the 1960s, and have been joined in recent years by others from across the continent who fuse African and Western rhythms, such as Ladysmith Black Mambazo from South Africa, Youssou

N'Dour of Senegal, Benin's Angelique Kidjo, and the late Fela Kuti of Nigeria. But few might imagine Bizet's *Carmen*, sung in a sassy, spirited style by a young diva from a poor black township near Cape Town. Pauline Malefane was plucked out of the chorus to star in the opera when the voice of the Swedish soprano brought to Cape Town for the performance didn't hold up against the lusty black voices in the chorus who had been recruited from around the country.

Malefane told me she learned the lead role in under three weeks, overcoming in the process her insecurities and doubts. After performing to great accolades in South Africa and later Europe, Malefane went on to star in the movie version, *U-Carmen e-Khayelitsha*, spoken and sung in Xhosa, one of South Africa's eleven official languages. The opera adapts the story to the life and rhythms of the township from which Malefane came, blending Xhosa culture with European opera. The film went on to win the Golden Bear Award for best film at the prestigious Berlin International Film Festival, only the second South African film in twenty-five years to be so honored.

Malefane's success does not obliterate the realities of the township in which she grew up, many of whose 1 million people are crammed into tiny shacks without electricity or running water, and many of whose young men and women have little education and no skills and are hanging out on street corners with no jobs or prospects. But the production of *U-Carmen* goes against the grain of negative perceptions, demonstrating that Africans have more to contribute than sad songs and sorrowful stories.

I have tried to drive home the importance of presenting a more balanced picture of the continent in my interaction with media decision makers in the United States, especially journalists of color who came into the profession in the wake of the 1968 Kerner Commission, which concluded that the predomi-

nantly white and male media industry had to bear some of the
blame for its failure to report on the conditions that caused the
rage that spilled over into the streets of America's inner cities in
the late sixties—poverty, lack of basic services, poor-quality
health care and education. Part of that failure was due to the fact
that few media institutions had working for them anyone who
looked like or lived with or near the people who were so enraged
and who could help the invisible be seen, the unheard be listened to. And no one in the "white" media ever went there,
except on the rare occasions when a sports figure set a record or
a criminal committed some horrendous crime. In the end, the
recommendations of the Kerner Commission, as it was known,
were adopted by the U.S. media, and the process of hiring more
people of color began in earnest so that the media could present
more accurate portrayals of people of color in all their complexity.[14] Led by legendary *Washington Post* journalist Robert C.
"Bob" Maynard, I joined other colleagues in a special acceler-
ated three-month program at Columbia University aimed at
rapidly increasing the number of minorities in the profession.
Those who passed through the program soon accounted for 20
percent of the black journalists in the newsrooms of America,
and over time they changed the face of American journalism—
literally and figuratively. Many of these journalists now hold top
editorial posts in the industry and are able to make decisions
about what gets covered and how.

Such individuals are also in a position to take the lead in
applying the same skills and commitment to changing the face of
international journalism that they used to change the face of
journalism in America. As huge as it is, Africa as a continent is
as invisible now as was black America in the U.S. media prior
to the riots of 1968, and the lesson learned from the Kerner
Commission is one that could and should be applied on the
African continent. It is one that African journalists are beginning

to insist on. It carries a set of challenges, but there are also great
potential rewards.

South African president Thabo Mbeki has told African journalists: "You were African before you became journalists and . . .
despite your profession, you are still Africans."[15] These words
and their meaning are and will be part of an ongoing debate as
African journalists find their anchor in sometimes stormy
African seas during this fragile period.

   South African journalists, for example, are not exempt from
their own history, in which the apartheid state had determined
what editorial content was unacceptable—including all coverage of its repression and brutality—and censored it. But there
were "guerrilla typewriters," and they told that story. For South
African journalists, no matter where they stood during apartheid, the Truth and Reconciliation Commission was a moment
of truth that helped put their history in a context, and set many
of them who had worked under apartheid strictures on editorial
course corrections that are still being pursued today. One of
the biggest challenges is striking a balance between giving the
young black-led government its just due as it implements
policies aimed at wiping out apartheid's inequities, and holding
it accountable for its actions across the board.

   South African journalists enjoy greater freedoms under their
constitution and greater resources than do journalists anywhere else on the continent. Ownership of the news media is
still concentrated in the hands of whites, but one of the largest
media companies, Johnnic Communications, is by a black
CEO, Connie Molusi. Additionally, black journalists have been
elevated to top editorial positions in the print media, as well
as at the state-owned South African Broadcasting Corporation
(SABC), which broadcasts both locally and around the continent and operates three commercial radio stations that broadcast
in eleven languages. During the apartheid era, the SABC was

controlled by the white minority government and reflected its racist politics. Since the black-led African National Congress government took power, the SABC has been accused of favoring it, although it does carry reports on government critics. Its Channel Africa has gained viewers and respect as it attempts to expand its content, as well as broaden the base of coverage beyond South Africa to make it more appealing to a wider variety of people in and beyond South Africa.

Launched in 1998, e.tv is the feisty entry into the South Africa media world—the only commercial television station to begin broadcasting since the end of apartheid. And while it doesn't have the resources or the reach of the SABC, it produces hard-hitting programs that go after corruption, as well as other stories that are not always flattering to government officials but defy traditional clichés.

The South African media are still in transition, with many of the new black editors, in particular, and journalists in general still finding their sea legs. But in international competitions on the continent, their submissions often stand head and shoulders above those from other countries.

Still, elsewhere in Africa, journalists are increasingly taking ownership of their stories, their progress measurable by many yardsticks. Ten years ago, Ghana-based lawyer Edward Boateng founded the CNN African Journalist of the Year Awards; in 2005 there were some 630 entries from forty countries, up from 465 from thirty countries the previous year. Moreover, African journalists are taking on more serious stories, including issues of human rights abuses, abuses of power, bribery and corruption, and other subjects that have been taboo in many African so-cieties, such as female circumcision, homosexuality, and the Catholic Church's stand on HIV/AIDS.

"African journalists are now being seen as the first line of defense when it comes to making sure there are checks and balances on their individual governments," I was told by CNN

Africa correspondent Jeff Koinange, who has served as a judge
for the awards Boateng started.

I am indebted to African journalists from Lagos to Addis Ababa
and points in between, who have unfailingly been there for me
with everything from coffee to context. They get paid to work as
translators and "fixers," those who help us with navigation and
contacts, even places to get a good meal or the best exchange rate,
but the added bonus for them is the sheer joy of joining in a journalistic enterprise that will reflect a reality closer to the truth
they know and live with every day.

One of my most vivid memories was of my first trip to Lagos
in 1998, when I was new to radio and to most of the continent.
Having survived the chatter-filled chaos of the bustling Lagos
airport, which surely was some sort of rite of passage, I made it
to my hotel and called a local journalist whose name had been
given to me by Jeri Eddings, who at the time was running the
Johannesburg office of Freedom Forum, a U.S.-based organization dedicated to freedom of the press around the world. Jeri
was in touch with often-beleaguered journalists all over the
continent, almost around the clock.

Within short order, Babafemi Ojudu had made his way across
Lagos and proceeded to give me a primer on everything I
needed to know about Nigeria—but with such modesty that
I had to learn from someone else the story of his arrest and
detention in solitary confinement for months on end during the
days of Sani Abacha, one of the most abusive and brutal of
Nigeria's long line of military rulers. Ojudu had been subjected
to nearly indescribable cruelty for doing his job as a journalist.
Once he was able to smuggle out some words about his condition:

I hardly sleep in the night. Since last Friday I have eaten
twice. I was not on hunger strike but my body is rejecting

the roadside food. Sometime I vomit soon after eating. I am now physically a wreck. I feel therefore I should appeal to you to see what you can do for me legally before it is too late. My fear is that these people may really be after my life.[16]

Ojudu invited me to the offices of his weekly paper, *The News*, to meet colleagues whom he thought could be helpful to me. I was totally unprepared for what I saw: reporters coming in from a story, preparing to write by pulling out paper from a huge roll on a desk in a room so small that the table on which the paper rested almost took up the entire room. The reporter would find a place to spread out the paper, then slowly craft the story, using a pencil. Later, the reporter would join the queue of reporters waiting to hand in their copy, prepared in the same fashion, to the typist, who sat at the one remaining computer the paper owned.

When I asked about this, I was told, "Oh yes, we had another computer, but Abacha's men confiscated it and, after taking it to the police station where they had also taken some of the reporters, deliberately left it out in the rain."

I also met Christiannah Oluwabukola Malaolu, the wife of another journalist, Niran Malaolu, who at the time was still in prison. He, too, had been arrested by the Abacha regime, and no one knew the reason. The prison was hours away from Lagos, so she could not visit often, but on the few occasions when she did, she found her husband's health steadily deteriorating; on one occasion his eyes were so infected, they feared he was going blind.

Later, when I met with the interim head of government, General Abdulsalami Abubakar, I raised the matter with him, saying that it was my understanding that all journalists detained during the Abacha regime should have been released. He didn't know Malaolu personally but expressed surprise that he was still in prison, and promised me he would look into it.

Months later, I got a message that Malaolu had indeed been released and was heading to Los Angeles for medical treatment. I gave him my daughter's phone number and told him to call her. After he did, Suesan arranged for him to meet some of her friends, fellow artists as well as actors and journalists, to talk about his ordeal and about changes in Nigeria. To my surprise, he told them I had been responsible for his freedom. I was moved, but I'm sure there were also others pressing on his behalf. Public pressure then, as now, is important and sometimes makes a difference.

Over the next four years, I would encounter more of the same, only in other places: brave men and women doing the work of journalism under circumstances that most of us could scarcely imagine. Few owned computers, but increasing numbers were able to gain access to e-mail and Web sites through Internet cafés. Likewise, while many of us who are international correspondents dip in and out of danger, danger is the common denominator in the lives of most African journalists on the continent.

Jeri Eddings told a group of Africans during a workshop on the New Partnership for African Development that "African journalists . . . [have been] murdered while attempting to cover stories, especially in conflict situations. At least 15 journalists were specifically targeted and murdered in Sierra Leone since 1997 and subsequently at least seven journalists received identical death threats of the sort that others had received before they were in fact murdered."[17] Many have been murdered for the "crime" of taking on corrupt regimes, including Gambian journalist Deyda Hydara, a widely read government critic and correspondent for Reporters Without Borders.

Still, murder is now taking a backseat to other forms of repression, as Yves Sorokobi, formerly with the New York-based Committee to Protect Journalists, has observed. "Instead of the heavy-handed ways they used in the past," he wrote, "dictators are using the laws of the country. They have a lot to hide, they have skeletons in their closet, but they can't get away with murder."[18]

In 2004, Sierra Leonean journalist Paul Kamara was sentenced to four years in prison for libel after being sued by the president. In recent years, African journalists have also had their outlets banned in Liberia, Gambia, Zambia, and Angola; Freedom House, a nonprofit group monitoring freedom and democracy around the world, still ranks those countries' media as "not free." And in aging regimes such as in Gabon, Cameroon, Lesotho, and Mauritania, "the plight of press freedom may be less dramatic," according to Reporters Without Borders, but "the authorities used their police, their army and their easily swayed judiciary to express their irritation with the media."[19]

Reporters Without Borders also chronicled the following media abuse around the continent in 2004:

In Paul Kagame's Rwanda, the state did not stop prosecuting the only really critical newspaper and its journalists were followed by government agents. In this country that was so tragically scarred by hate media in the past, press freedom is virtually inexistent.

(I spoke with President Kagame in New York City about this during the UN General Assembly session in September 2005, and he promised to hold a further meeting on this matter.)

Opposition journalists were often thrown into jail in Sudan under repressive laws that permit inordinately long periods of preventive custody.

Even if the independent press including the satirical press was allowed a little leeway, Lansana Conté's Guinea still harassed some independent journalists and often censored newspapers that irked a strict and inflexible National Council of Communication. In Equatorial Guinea, the powerful pro-government press constantly attacked the weak opposition, if need be, exploiting racial prejudices.

In Swaziland, a poor little kingdom ruled by an eccentric young king, the staff of the state media had to sing the regime's praises on pain of dismissal.

The situation was paradoxical in Tanzania, where a reasonable degree of respect for press freedom on the mainland contrasted with the behavior of the authoritarian government running the semi-autonomous island of Zanzibar, which never stopped trying to throttle the weekly *Dira*, the island's only independent newspaper, until it was finally forced to close.

Zanzibar has parallels with Seychelles where the opposition weekly *Regar* was often assailed by the judiciary, and with Djibouti where the weekly *Le Renouveau* was constantly harassed by the government. In Madagascar, the overlapping of politics and news media is a source of problems and court actions against certain opposition radio stations continued to cast a shadow over an otherwise relatively free climate.[20]

Zimbabwe, labeled by the Committee to Protect Journalists as "one of the worst places to be a journalist" in 2004 and placed in Freedom House's "not free" category, is one of the best examples of a government using "a veneer of legality" to muzzle the press.[21]

And while all foreign journalists had been kicked out by the end of 2004, local journalists remained engaged in a running battle with the powers that be over legislation aimed at restricting their activities and their access to information.

Beginning in 2003, the government closed all of the independent media voices in the country, including Zimbabwe's only independent daily, the *Daily News*, which had a readership of some 1.5 million in a country of 11.6 million, leaving the public with only state-run or state-supported outlets. During the parliamentary elections of 2005, the government granted visas to a limited number of international journalists but continued its ban on the BBC, which it regarded as an instrument of its archenemy and former colonial ruler, Tony Blair's Britain.

I was allowed in and had a one-time experience that gave me deeper insight into some of the problems local journalists face on a regular basis. I was welcomed by an article in the state-controlled *Sunday Mail*, which said that "in the past [Charlayne Hunter-Gault] constantly churned out rabidly anti-Government pieces."[22] Later, when I challenged George Charamba, the secretary of information and publicity and the president's spokesman, he complained about a story I had done in 2004 about Zimbabweans being deported for being in South Africa illegally, most of whom had been working at any jobs they could find to help support families back home. In that story, which was filmed during an eighteen-hour train ride from the Lindela Detention Camp outside Johannesburg to the Zimbabwe border at the Beit Bridge, my colleagues Cynde Strand and Chevan Rayson captured with their cameras many of the Zimbabwean detainees jumping off the train during the night. On camera, I asked what could be so bad in Zimbabwe that it would drive people to jump from a moving train. The Zimbabwean men and women on the train told of political persecution and beatings, and of the economic hardship brought on by skyrocketing inflation and food priced beyond the reach of a country with an unemployment rate upwards of 70 percent.

Later I tried to get the government's response to its critics, but my efforts were fruitless.

On Election Day 2005, I ran into conflict with the Zimbabwean authorities. I was eager to see if there would be a repeat of the chaotic presidential election of 2002, where voters had stood in line so long that many had had friends bring their breakfast, lunch, and dinner. Many had slept on the sidewalk when the one-day voting period was extended to two. Even so, some voters still had been unable to cast their ballots. This time, the government redrew (critics say "gerrymandered") the district lines and added more polling stations. But when I arrived at the gate of a polling station in a densely populated district of Harare—the only area in the country won by the opposition in the 2002 election—I was surprised to see just a few voters. When I tried to get inside, using the credentials I had paid the Ministry of Information $600 for, a police officer insisted I needed still another credential. My tape recorder was confiscated, with the police officer insisting that I was violating the law by recording him. I persisted in telling him that I was doing neither. Four hours and two police stations later, I found myself sitting with criminals in a tiny room, waiting for the conclusion of an investigation the deputy inspector insisted had to be conducted before he could decide on the disposition of my case. One of the police officers involved in my detention told me as I was being "escorted" to the second police station, "I've seen what you do on TV." I didn't press him for details.

Fortunately for me, I was later released, my equipment returned. Two London-based journalists were not so lucky. They were arrested on the same day and charged with working without accreditation under a Zimbabwe law many media organizations have called "draconian," the Access to Information and Protection of Privacy Act (AIPPA), which requires all journalists to register with the government-controlled Media and Information Commission (MIC). They remained in prison for several days and were brought to court on several occasions in handcuffs. When they were eventually released, they were expelled from the country.

Some of the other three hundred or so foreign journalists permitted to cover the parliamentary elections were also briefly detained; a Swedish reporter was deported, despite his accreditation, while dozens were refused entry because the Zimbabwean government regarded them as hostile to the state. The BBC was denied, according to the government's Charamba, because "they already perceive the elections are not free and fair."

After my release, I came across some local journalists from the *Daily News*, which at that point had been shut for some seventeen months by the Media and Information Commission. The MIC insisted the closure was because the publishers of the *Daily News* refused to comply with the law, and it defended its tough media laws on the grounds that independent journalists had been irresponsible and had failed to police themselves. The *Daily News* insisted it had been shut down because of its editorial positions critical of the government. The case against the paper took two years before it was heard in court, without a final resolution. The paper is still banned, though it publishes online, with its reporters preparing their stories undercover and slipping into Internet cafés at odd hours to upload their material.

When I was in police custody, some local journalists heard about my detention and rushed to the police station. They worked for independent newspapers shut by the government, which called them "traitors" and "terrorists." After I was released and we had a chance to talk, the journalists told me they had written stories about beatings of opposition supporters, illegal torture of opposition activists, and state-encouraged farm seizures that had resulted in the murder of a dozen commercial farmers and the displacement of thousands of black farm workers.

"We were documenting all of this," Precious Shumba of the *Daily News* told me. "And our newspaper is a moving piece of history, where anyone willing to understand the facts can go back to our archives and check what we did, and the government was angered by that. And the government remains committed to the banishment of newspapers like ours."[23]

Commenting about my detention, another *Daily News* journalist, Stanley Gama, told me: "It happens to us all the time." Both he and Shumba had been detained on previous occasions, questioned for up to six hours, and released. So have many others, though none has yet been charged.

"Some of my colleagues were tortured, severely tortured," Gama told me. "Some had to go for treatment outside the country. I know of one female photographer who was assaulted severely by these security agents."[24]

I asked if the two if they weren't afraid to be associating with me, since under the media law it was a crime for a Zimbabwean journalist to work for a foreign news organization. They pointed out that they were not working for me as journalists, but I was concerned that if the law was as arbitrary as it seemed, they could possibly be detained for guilt by association.

"I'm not scared," Gama told me, "because I believe if you want to fight these laws like AIPPA, we have to do it from within. We have to show some form of resistance so they know it's a bad law. Running away is not a solution. So we have to face this draconian law here, so hopefully we will be able to succeed."[25]

This defiant spirit is in full flower in other parts of the continent as well, including what Reporters Without Borders referred to as "dismembered" states such as Somalia. There, where a civil war that erupted in 1991 has left the country in lawless chaos, "several privately-owned radio stations and newspapers continue to inform the public and maintain the links of common language and social life that unite a population otherwise abandoned to itself and anarchy."[26]

Nowhere is the spirit of Africa's second wind more vibrant and producing more new news than in Ghana, where African journalists took a great step forward in 2000, as the country was about to hold the first democratic change of power in the nineteen years of the country's postcolonial history.

Popular radio journalist Kwaku Sakyi-Addo participated in the first-ever presidential debate, organized by the Freedom Forum's Jeri Eddings, who tapped me to moderate it. The well-attended event drew all but one of the nine presidential candidates, as well as the applause and often spirited comments of a nation grateful, as was I, to be in on this historic moment.

Moreover, on Election Day it was Ghana's journalists who called in from their cell phones to radio talk shows, reporting gross irregularities in the election, even identifying by name a government agent who was stealing ballot boxes. If you don't think that was brave, let me hasten to tell you that he was armed and they weren't, except with the truth, which wouldn't stop a bullet.

Four years later, in the next election, Ghanaian journalists once again helped deepen the country's democratic roots, fanning out to polling stations around the country and reporting vote counts over the airwaves, narrowing the space for dirty tricks.

As the space for more independent media voices has grown, so has the power of radio, being used increasingly as a voice for the voiceless, stirring up passion for freedom and human fulfillment. In 1985, there were only about three hundred radio stations on the entire continent. Today, there are close to two thousand. And as they proliferate, so do the calls for more programming in indigenous languages. As Tawana Kupe, head of the School of Literature, Languages and Media Studies at the

University of the Witwatersrand in South Africa, has said: "A large majority of Africans (including the 'educated' ones) best understand communication in their own languages."[27]

Many Africans already in journalism traveled a hard road, with little training or encouragement, their passion for the profession fueled only by the fire that burned inside them to do this thing we call journalism. A good number went directly into the profession from secondary school, never having had an economics course or other formal education that would help them unravel the complexities of a continent struggling to enter the new global economy. In many countries, including Nigeria, there are few resources for training both the beginners and the many veteran African journalists who now need greater insights into the details and machinations of the global economic arena that Africa desperately needs to be a part of. Also, African journalists have a crying need for modern technology. The digital divide is real and limits the capacity of the African journalists to inform their readers at this critical time in the development of the continent.

Also critical to the emergence of a new generation of journalists is assistance to those who are emerging from under the yoke of state control of the media. How to be watchdogs and not lapdogs is a lesson that needs to be learned. African journalists' pay is still so notoriously low that over the years they have been easy prey for corrupt politicians who have used their own ill-gotten gains to pay for positive stories about themselves or prevent negative ones—stories of brown paper bags stuffed with cash abound. This is not to say that all journalists on the continent have been corrupted; quite the contrary. Many have resisted, and struggle to make ends meet, but remain determined to do their jobs with professionalism and dignity. But bribery continues to be a problem, as does journalists' pay.

"Ethics, I can say, is on the lowest ebb," Nigeria's Babafemi Ojudu told me in mid-2005. "There is so much corruption at the level of both the reporters and the editors. One is apprehensive about the future of the profession. The economic situation here and the dwindling readership . . . are pretty responsible."[28]

Ojudu said he was worried that many of the journalists are in the profession "not because they have flair or passion for it, but because there is not opportunity elsewhere. Those with flair zare leaving to find something more lucrative to do." He did say, however, that the environment has changed for the better: "The fear of harassment, jail, or threat of jail is no longer there."[29]

As African journalists attempt to take more control of how Africans are portrayed in the media, new organizations on the continent are springing up to support them in reporting abuses and also in training and development. Moreover, the Commission for Africa, set up by British Prime Minister Tony Blair to look at the scope of African problems, recommended donors "increase substantially their funding to African independent media institutions and those governments promoting free media."[30]

But some are going beyond these ideas, including Moeletsi Mbeki, a South African businessman (and brother of the current president) who was a journalist while he was in exile, and Salim Amin, son of the late, widely heralded journalist and cameraman Mohammed Amin. Both men argued for resources to establish and support African-owned continent-wide news organs. Said Mbeki: "If we want to get our story out there, we have to get ourselves out there. That's the big challenge. We have to find a way to make the media commercially viable in Africa because donor funding is not sustainable—it is too temporary and too controlling. Their agenda is not always our agenda, especially in a postcolonial, postapartheid era."[31]

The debate over Thabo Mbeki's admonition to African journalists to be "Africans first" continues to generate soul-searching as
African journalists keep on uncovering the building blocks of
the African renaissance. To some, calling on African journalists
to remember that they are Africans first may sound like a call to
patriotism. But what does being patriotic mean for a journalist?
And should patriotism be defined differently in the developing
world than in, say, the United States of America post-9/11?

Zimbabwe's independent journalists and their counterparts
in Ghana, Benin, and elsewhere have defined their role and their
patriotism in the same way, seeing themselves as guardians of the
interests of the people and not the powers that be, working to
entrench not leaders but their democracy, insisting on account-
ability and transparency in the government and in the political
process—and, for a growing number, themselves and their institutions. These patriots are assessing their governments' record
by the promises they make to their citizens and the ones they
keep. And that's part of the "new news" out of Africa. If this
spirit is nurtured and supported, Africans won't be the only
beneficiaries. The war on terrorism knows no boundaries, as
does the recruitment of terrorists who are likely to find as much
fertile ground among the ignorant and poor and desperate as
they do among fanatical religious zealots.

Some African journalists have argued that they should not be
following Western media models. "African stories get told to
Africans by North Americans and Europeans with the same
subtle ideological manipulations as in the colonial era," educator
Tawana Kupe insists. But I think that criticism arises partly out of
the way in which they've seen the Western media portray them
and their continent, and also from the examples they've seen of
Western media being mouthpieces for their own governments,
particularly in the wake of 9/11 and the invasion of Iraq. I argue
that African journalists can take issue with the practices of

Western journalism, but not with the principles of fairness and balance and telling the truth as they see it.

The debate about African journalists being "Africans first" is a good thing, as it helps journalists on the continent keep in the forefront of their minds how best to present information that is accurate and fair and assists their countries to develop on behalf of their people. In my view, being "African first" means that African journalists report through the prism of their own experiences.

At an editor's conference in Johannesburg in 2003, editors from around the continent called for better coverage of the African story from African perspectives and more news exchanges within Africa. They also called on state media to become independent public service media, rather than government mouthpieces.

At the same time, African journalists will surely want to demand of their leaders, especially those who've embraced NEPAD, the continent-wide program that promotes good governance and sound economic management, that they guarantee journalists the freedom to do their jobs. The 1981 African Charter on Human and Peoples' Rights guarantees press freedom, but there is no provision for enforcing it against recalcitrant governments, as Yves Sorokobi, formerly of the Committee to Protect Journalists, has pointed out.[32] And in 1991 a UN-sponsored meeting in Windhoek, Namibia, produced a document that defined a free press as "independent from governmental, political or economic control or from control of materials and infrastructure essential for the production and dissemination of newspapers, magazines and periodicals."[33] But the African Union's Constitutive Act, from 2002, did not specifically address the issue of media freedom.

African journalists are eager to be instrumental in helping create the African renaissance, but its promise rests on a fragile compact with a new generation of leaders who have beckoned them toward that renaissance—which is still more of a rallying cry than a concrete reality.

The world in which the African journalist operates is in the process of becoming, and African journalists have a duty to report it—the birth pangs as well as the first baby steps of the continent's new democracies. African journalists thus become one of the main guardians of their new world as it is aborning, ensuring that the African people have the information they need to nurture the continent's growth and development, and protect it from any who would do it harm. For this reason it is essential to encourage young Africans with dreams of becoming journalists to realize those dreams.

I am often reminded of my own desire to become a journalist, back in a time when young black girls growing up in the segregated South were not supposed to have such dreams. When I told my mother of my dreams, inspired by the comic strip character Brenda Starr, she didn't tell me to can the pipe dreams and do something real. She simply said, "If that's what you want to do, fine," for instinctively my mother knew that dreams propel ambition. As a result, my life as a journalist has exceeded even my wildest dreams.

If we encourage African journalists, their stories—told from their own experiences—will surely give rise to a new generation of Africans, and also to a new generation of the world's people who may live beyond the continent's borders but who, thanks to the work of African journalists, will understand the continent in a way that will help them to embrace it as the mother of us all.

# Notes

## Chapter One: South Africa, Then and Now

1. James A. Emanuel and Theodore L. Gross, *Dark Symphony: Negro Literature in America* (New York: Free Press, 1968).
2. Noel Mostert, *Frontiers* (New York: Alfred A. Knopf, 1992), xxi.
3. Salih Booker, "The Colour Line: US Foreign Policy and National Interests in Africa," *South African Journal of International Affairs* 8, 1 (2001), 11.
4. Charlayne Hunter-Gault, *In My Place* (New York: Vintage, 1992), 210–11.
5. Booker, "The Colour Line," 12.
6. W. E. B. Du Bois, *The Souls of Black Folks* (New York: Fawcett, 1964), 17.
7. Nelson Mandela, *Long Walk to Freedom* (London: Abacus, 1995), 681–82.
8. Ibid., 682.
9. Ibid.
10. Ibid., 680.
11. www.UNICEF.org/specialsession/activities/nelson-mandela-bio.htm. (Graca Machel early on established herself as an

advocate for children while serving as Mozambique's first minister of education after independence, penning the book *The Impact of War on Children* (London: Hurst, 2001).

12. F. W. de Klerk, interview by Charlayne Hunter-Gault for the *MacNeil/Lehrer NewsHour*, April 29, 1994.

13. Nelson Mandela, interview by Charlayne Hunter-Gault for the *MacNeil/Lehrer NewsHour*, May 6, 1994.

14. Alex Boraine, *A Country Unmasked: Inside South Africa's Truth and Reconciliation Commission* (New York: Oxford University Press, 2001), 99.

15. Charlayne Hunter-Gault, Introduction to Antjie Krog, *Country of My Skull: Guilt, Sorrow, and the Limits of Forgiveness in the New South Africa* (New York: Times Books, 1999), x.

16. Allister Sparks, *Beyond the Miracle: Inside the New South Africa* (Jeppestown, South Africa: Jonathan Ball, 2003), 163.

17. Antjie Krog, *Country of My Skull: Guilt, Sorrow, and the Limits of Forgiveness in the New South Africa* (New York: Times Books, 1999), 80.

18. Ibid., 148.

19. Lynne Duke, *Mandela, Mobutu and Me* (New York: Doubleday, 1994), 107.

20. www.suthafrica.info/what_happening/news/apartheid-lawsuits.htm.

21. Thabo Mbeki speech to the National House of Parliament and the Nation, at the Tabling of the Report of the Truth and Reconciliation Commission, April 15, 2003; www.info.gov.za/speeches/2003/03041514011003.htm.

22. Interview by Charlayne Hunter-Gault for CNN, April 18, 2003.

23. www.globalpolicy.org/intljustice/atca/2005/0106khulumani.htm.

24. In November 2005 three mass graves were found accidentally by construction workers. They were believed to be

those of Namibian guerrillas who fought against the South
African occupation of their country until 1990. Such dis-
coveries gave hope to families in South Africa, even as it
caused more outrage against the old apartheid regime.
"Mass Grave Horror," *The Star* (Johannesburg), November
11, 2005.

25. Interview by Charlayne Hunter-Gault, March 2004.
26. Ibid.
27. *Mail and Guardian* (Johannesburg), April 22–28, 2005, 10.
28. www.unaids.org/epi2005/doc/download.html.
29. Futhi Ntshingila, "Under Cover of Darkness," *Sunday Times* (Johannesburg), January 30, 2005, 19.
30. Angela Quintal, "Break Silence on Disease of Racism—Mbeki," *Cape Times*, October 22, 2004.
31. Ibid.
32. Jon Jeter, "South Africa's Advances Jeopardized by AIDS," *Washington Post*, July 6, 2000.
33. Ibid.
34. Ibid.
35. Ibid.
36. Thabo Mbeki, interview, CNN, June 24, 2004.
37. Ibid.
38. Peter Slevin, "Mbeki Says Diplomacy Needed for Zimbabwe," *Washington Post*, September 25, 2003.
39. Mangosuthu Buthelezi, interview by Charlayne Hunter-Gault for CNN, January 14, 2005.
40. Helmo Preuss, "Vodafone Deal Great for SA," November 4, 2005, http://business.iafrica.com/news/526010.htm.
41. Brian Brink, interview by Charlayne Hunter-Gault, June 2005.
42. Ibid.
43. "Affirmative Action in Higher Education: The United States and South Africa," symposium held at the University

of Michigan, April 14–15, 2005, Charlayne Hunter-Gault's notes from informal remarks by Justice Yvonne Mokgoro.

44. Mandela, *Long Walk to Freedom*, 3.

45. Interview by Charlayne Hunter-Gault for CNN, March 4, 2004.

46. Ibid.

47. Henriette Geldenhuys, "Needy Students Get a Reprieve," *Sunday Times* (Johannesburg), May 2, 2004, www.suntimes.co.za/2004/05/02/news/gauteng/njhb06.asp.

48. Loyiso Nongxa, vice chancellor, University of the Witwatersrand, "Letter to Parents," December 13, 2004.

49. Taddy Bletcher, e-mail to Charlayne Hunter-Gault, November 15, 2005.

50. Thabo Mbeki, comments at the Enterprise Development Forum, March 6, 2004; *Financial Mail*, February 25, 2005.

51. Ernst and Young (Johannesburg), "Mergers & Acquisitions, Review of Activity for the Year 2005—14th Edition"; *Business Day* (Johannesburg), April 8, 2005.

52. "Against Cronyism," *Mail and Guardian* (Johannesburg), November 11–17, 2005.

53. Moeletsi Mbeki, interview by Charlayne Hunter-Gault, November 14, 2005.

54. Lionel October, phone interview by Charlayne Hunter-Gault, November 18, 2005.

55. Saki Macozoma, interview by Charlayne Hunter-Gault, December 3, 2004.

56. Reg Romney, phone interview by Charlayne Hunter-Gault, November 14, 2005.

57. "BEE Code to Boost 'Mixed' Businesses," *Business Day* (Johannesburg), October 31, 2005.

58. Helgard van Wyk, "National Personal Income of South Africans by Population Group, Income, Life Stage and

Life Plane, 1960–2007," Report 333, Bureau of Market Research, University of South Africa, 2004.

59. Ibid.

60. Thabo Mbeki, speech to South African Women Entrepreneurs Network, May 12, 2005, www.southafrica.info/women/mbeki-women-120505.htm.

61. Reg Romney, interview by Charlayne Hunter-Gault, June 2, 2005.

62. Wendy Luhabe, telephone interview by Charlayne Hunter-Gault, June 6, 2004.

63. South African Advertising Research Foundation, AMPS Survey, 2005.

64. Ciko Thomas, interview by Charlayne Hunter-Gault, December 9, 2004.

65. Ibid.

66. Sampie Terreblanche, *A History of Inequality in South Africa* (Pietermaritzburg: University of Natal Press, 2002), 13–14.

67. Ciko Thomas, interview by Charlayne Hunter-Gault, December 9, 2004.

68. South African Labour and Development Research Unit, University of Cape Town, October Household Survey (OHS) and Labour Force Survey (LFS), data from Statistical Releases of Statistics South Africa, www.cssr.uct.ac.za/saldru.html.

69. Medical Research Council, University of Cape Town, and the Center for the Study of Violence and Reconciliation Policy Brief, June 2004.

70. Ed Stoddard, "S. Africa Woman Killed by Partner Every 6 Hours—Study," Reuters, May 24, 2005.

71. Rachel Jewkes, Loveday Penn-Kekana, and Hetty Rose-Junius, "'If They Rape Me, I Can't Blame Them': Reflections on Gender in the Social Context of Child Rape

in South Africa and Namibia," *Social Science and Medicine* 61, 8 (2005), 1809–20.

72. Gareth Newham, telephone interview by Charlayne Hunter-Gault , May 26, 2005.

73. Thabo Mbeki, speech to the National Assembly, June 10, 1997.

74. Thabo Mbeki, speech to the Constitutional Assembly, May 8, 1996; International Marketing Council of South Africa, April 2005.

75. Charlayne Hunter-Gault's files.

76. David Lamb, *The Africans* (London: Methuen, 1985).

77. International Marketing Council of South Africa, April 2005.

78. "Statement of the President of South Africa, Thabo Mbeki, at the Joint Sitting of Parliament on the Release of Hon. Jacob Zuma from His Responsibilities as Deputy President: National Assembly," June 14, 2005, www.ipocafrica.org/cases/armsdeal/shaik/mbeki140605.pdf.

79. Institute for Security Studies, Southern African Information Portal on Corruption, "The State vs. Shabir Shaik and 11 Others," www.ipocafrica.org/cases/armsdeal/shaik.

80. Research Surveys, "What Do People Really Think About the Zuma Affair?" www.biz-community.com/Article/196/19/8358.html.

81. www.info.gov.za/speeches/2005/05060916151003.htm.

82. Dominic Mahlangu Wisini Wa Ka Ngonbeni and Dumasani Lubiosi. *The Sunday Times* (Johannesburg), November 13, 2005, "Zuma Rape Claim." He was later charged.

83. www.dfa.gov.za/docs/speeches/2005/mbek0802.htm.

84. Martin Luther King Jr., quoted on www.nathanielturner.com/martinlutherking.htm.

Chapter Two: Baby Steps to Democracy

1. Thomas Pakenham, *The Scramble for Africa* (New York: Random House, 1991), 675.
2. Patrice Lumumba, "Weep, O Beloved Black Brother," www.africawithin.com/lumumba/patrice_lumumba.htm.
3. William Cullen Bryant, "The Battle-Field," www.bartleby.com/73/1829.html.
4. www-africa2015.org/factspoverty.pdf.
5. Thabo Mbeki, speech at the launch of the African Union, July 9, 2002, www.anc.org.za/ancdocs/history/mbeki/2002/tm0709.html.
6. Ibid.
7. Wamba dia Wamba, e-mail to Charlayne Hunter-Gault, May 4, 2005.
8. Adam Hochschild, *King Leopold's Ghost* (Boston: Mariner Books, 1999), 303.
9. BBC News, "Country Profile: Burundi," http://news.bbc.co.uk/1/hi/world/africa/country_profiles/1068873.stm.
10. BBC News, "France's Ivorian Quagmire," http://news.bbc.co.uk/1/hi/world/africa/3993265.stm.
11. Richard Mantu, "Mbeki in Ivory Coast Breakthrough," April 7, 2005, www.southafrica.info/what_happening/news/african_union/ivorycoast-070405.htm.
12. Institute for Security Studies, "Nigeria: Population," www.iss.co.za/AF/profiles/Nigeria/Population.html.
13. Transparency International, "Nine Out of Ten Developing Countries Urgently Need Practical Support to Fight Corruption, Highlights New Index," www.transparency.org/pressreleases_archive/2003/2003.10.07.cpi.en.html.
14. http://allafrica.com/stories/printable/200510170893.html.

15. Bola A. Akinterinwa, "On Buhari's Mass Action," www. thisdayonline.com/archive/2003/05/26/20030526com01. html.

16. The European observer Max Van Den Berg noted, "Many instances of ballot box stuffing, just bluntly in the face of our observers, a lot of times even without hiding anything; changing of results and other serious irregularities," "Democracy's Challenge," *NewsHour with Jim Lehrer*, May 1, 2003, www.pbs.org/newshour/bb/africa/jan-june03/ nigeria_05-01.html.

17. "Democracy's Challenge," *NewsHour with Jim Lehrer*, May 1, 2003, www.pbs.org/newshour/bb/africa/jan-june03/ nigeria_05-01.html.

18. "Statement by the African Union Observer/Monitoring Team on the 2003 Presidential, Gubernatorial and National Assembly Elections in the Federal Republic of Nigeria," April 22, 2003, www.dfa.gov.za/docs/2003/au0422.htm.

19. Kola Ologbond, "Commonwealth, Mandela, African Leaders Congratulate Obasanjo," www.thisdayonline.com/ archive/ 2003/04/25/20030425news04.html.

20. Thompson Akpogo, "Togo Rivals Agree in Nigeria to Accept Outcome of Vote," Associated Press, April 25, 2005.

21. Bryan Mealer, "Election Results Spark Riots in Togo," Associated Press, April 27, 2005.

22. Interview by Charlayne Hunter-Gault, CNN, June 4, 2003.

23. CNN, "Mugabe: Democracy Was the Winner," http:// archives.cnn.com/2002/WORLD/africa/03/17/zimbabwe. mugabe; Ofeibea Quist-Arcton, "Commonwealth Observers Sharply Critical of Election," http://allafrica.com/stories/ 200203140772.html.

24. www.kubatana.net/html/archive/legisl/020122posad.asp?sec tor=LEGISL&range_start+1#23.

25. Amnesty International, "Zimbabwe: Rights Under Siege," document index no. AFR 46/012/2003, May 2, 2003, http://web.amnesty.org/library/index/engafr460122003.

26. Ibid.

27. Diana Games, "A Pre-Election Overview and Recovery Scenarios in Zimbabwe," March 14, 2005, South African Institute for International Affairs, www.ijr.org.za/transitionaljustice/zim/saiiapre.

28. Reuters, "Bicycle Boom Pushes Zimbabwe Inflation to 411 Pct," www.zwnews.com/issuefull.cfm?ArticleID=13167.

29. "Zimbabwe: Economy," CIA World Factbook, www.cia.gov/cia/publications/factbook/geos/zi.html#Econ.

30. Games, "A Pre-Election Overview."

31. U.S. Agency for International Development, Famine Early Warning Systems Network (FewsNet), "New Harvest Brings Limited Relief," Zimbabwe Food Security Update, March 30, 2005, www.fews.net/centers/files/Zimbabwe_200502en.pdf.

32. Peta Thornycroft, "Wheels Come Off in Zimbabwe," *Sunday Independent* (Johannesburg), May 1, 2005, www.iol.co.za/index.php?set_id=1&click_id=68&art_id=vn20050501103352311C767385.

33. UNICEF, "Zimbabwe's Forgotten Children," March 17, 2005, www.unicef.org/infobycountry/zimbabwe_25622.html.

34. UN Special Envoy on Human Settlements Issues in Zimbabwe, UN Human Settlements Programme, "Report of the Fact-Finding Mission to Assess the Scope and Impact of Operation Murambatsvina," July 18, 2005, www.unhabitat.org/documents/ZimbabweReport.pdf.

35. "Sister Walsh's Account," ZWNews.com, posted June 3, 2005, www.zwnews.com/issuefull.cfm?ArticleID=12021.

36. Chris Fomunyoh, interview with Charles Ako of Radio Equinox, Douala, Cameroon, December 6, 2002.

37. Muammar Ghadaffi, interview by Charlayne Hunter-Gault for CNN, July 14, 2002.

38. South African foreign minister, Nkosana Dhamini-Zuma, interview by Charlayne Hunter-Gault for CNN, December 21, 2000.

39. Pan-African Parliament's Constitutive Act, July 11, 2000, Lome, Togo.

40. Prince Mashele, interview by Charlayne Hunter-Gault, May 5, 2005.

41. Ibid.

42. Jon Corzine and Richard Holbrooke, "Help the African Union," *Washington Post*, September 9, 2004.

43. Prince Mashale, interview by Charlayne Hunter-Gault, May 5, 2005.

44. Christopher Fomunyoh, "African Solutions to African Problems: A Slogan Whose Time Has Passed," AllAfrica. com, February 9, 2005, http://allafrica.com/stories/ 200502090005.html.

45. John Stremlau, telephone interview with Charlayne Hunter-Gault, May 24, 2005.

46. Lucy Ward, " 'Missionary' Blair's African Crusade," *The Guardian* (London), February 1, 2002, http://politics.guardian. co.uk/foreignaffairs/story/0,11538,642774,00.html.

47. Mark Tran, "US Opposes UK's Debt Relief Plan," *The Guardian* (London), February 4, 2005, www.guardian. co.uk/g8/story/0,13365,1406107,00.html.

48. Celia W. Dugger, "Discerning a New Course for World's Donor Nations," *New York Times*, April 18, 2005.

49. "Crumbs for Africa," editorial, *New York Times*, June 8, 2005.

50. "President Discusses G8 Summit, Progress in Africa," June 30, 2005, www.whitehouse.gov/news/releases/2005/ 06/20050630.html.

51. World Bank annual report, African Development Indicators, 2005. Foreword page, www.worldbank.org/afr/stats/adi2005/default.cfm.

52. www.50years.org/factsheets/Africa.html.

53. Quoted in Paul Jimbo and Benson Kathuri, "G8 Urged to Relieve Africa of Debt Burden," *The Standard* (Nairobi), May 2, 2005.

54. Salih Booker, telephone interview by Charlayne Hunter-Gault, June 9, 2005.

55. "The Debt Crisis," Data 2005, www.data.org/whyafrica/issuedebt.php.

56. Shadrack Gutto, telephone interview by Charlayne Hunter-Gault, June 10, 2005.

57. Ibid.

58. "Statement by the President of the United Nations General Assembly, H. E. Mr. Jan Eliasson, at the Opening of the Plenary Debate on the New Partnership for Africa's Development (NEPAD) and on the Decade to Roll Back Malaria," October 13, 2005, www.un.org/ga/president/60/speeches/051013.pdf.

59. Peter Fabricius, "Over Half Removed by Coup, War or Invasion," *The Star* (Johannesburg), November 18, 2005.

60. Ibid.

61. "ZANU-PF, MDC Friendly Heals Wounds," Zim Observer News Network, May 13, 2005, http://zimobserver.com/newsdetail.asp?article_id=1120.

62. Bamako Declaration of the African Statesmen Initiative, June 8, 2005, www.maliembassy-addis.org/ais.htm.

63. Chris Fomunyoh, telephone interview by Charlayne Hunter-Gault, June 1, 2005.

## Chapter Three: Reporting Renaissance

1. *The Economist*, May 13–19, 2000.
2. Gwen Lister, speech at SANEF All Africa Editors' Conference, Johannesburg, April 11–13, 2003.
3. Philippe Wamba, *Kinship* (New York: Dutton, 1999), 133.
4. Charlayne Hunter-Gault, "Charlayne in Africa," *Georgia Magazine*, June 1999, available at www.uga.edu/gm/699/FeatChar.html.
5. Ibid.
6. Hunter-Gault, "Charlayne in Africa." See also www.npr.org/templates/story/story.php?storyId=1033284.
7. Keith Richburg, *Out of Africa: A Black Man Confronts Africa* (New York: Basic Books, 1997), xii.
8. Hunter-Gault, "Charlayne in Africa."
9. Audio of Clinton's remarks at www.npr.org/templates/story/story.php?storyId=1035645.
10. UNAIDS, "Sub-Saharan Africa: HIV and AIDS Statistics and Features, end of 2002 and 2004," www.unaids.org/wad 2004/EPIupdate2004_html_en/epi04_05_en.htm.
11. UNAIDS, "South Africa," www.unaids.org/en/geographical+area/by+country/south+africa.asp.
12. AVERT, "HIV & AIDS Statistics for Africa," www.avert.org/subaadults.htm; United Nations News Centre, "AIDS Orphans in Sub-Saharan Africa: A Looming Threat to Future Generations," www.un.org/events/ tenstories/story.asp?storyID=400.
13. Mabaso family, interview by Charlayne Hunter-Gault for CNN, February 29, 2000.
14. "'The Communications Media, Ironically, Have Failed to Communicate': The Kerner Report Assesses Media Coverage of Riots and Race Relations," History Matters, www.historymatters.gmu.edu/d/6553.

15. Thabo Mbeki, comments at SANEF All Africa Editors' Conference, Johannesburg, April 12, 2003.

16. IFEX Alert, "Babafemi Ojundu Is Sick with Typhoid, Jaundice; Writes Will in Detention," July 23, 1998, www. ifex.org/en/content/view/full/6777.

17. Jerri Eddings, "Media Challenges Across Africa," NEPAD Communications and Marketing Workshop, January 28, 2002.

18. Matthew Green, "African Rulers Toughen Laws to Muzzle Press," Reuters, May 2, 2002.

19. Reporters Without Borders, "Continent of Hope and Death," Africa annual report 2005, www.rsf.org/ rubrique. php3?id_rubrique=510.

20. Ibid.

21. "Zimbabwe: Independent News Directors Arrested," Committee to Protect Journalists, September 22, 2003, www.cpj.org/news/2003/Zim22sept03na.html.

22. *The Sunday Mail*, March 27, 2005.

23. Interview by Charlayne Hunter-Gault for NPR, April 2005; broadcast based on this material available at www.npr.org/templates/story/story.php?storyId=4587011.

24. Ibid.

25. Ibid.

26. Reporters Without Borders, "Continent of Hope and Death."

27. Tawana Kupe, "Nothing African About It," *The Media* (South Africa), January 4, 2005, www.themedia.co.za/article.aspx? articleid=194638&area=/media_columnistsundercurrent.

28. Babafemi Ojundu, e-mail to Charlayne Hunter-Gault, June 9, 2005.

29. Ibid.

30. "Our Common Interest," Report of the Commission for Africa, March 11, 2005, p. 143, www.commissionfor

africa.org/english/report/thereport/english/11-03-05_cr_
report.pdf.

31. Moeletsi Mbeki, telephone interview by Charlayne Hunter-Gault, May 25, 2005.

32. Yves Sorokobi, Committee to Protect Journalists Report, Attacks on the Press in 2002, www.cpj.org/attacks02/africa02/africa.html.

33. Windhoek Declaration, May 3, 1991.

# Index

sexual assault, 38, 59–60, 63,
   67–68
Sexwale, Tokyo, 22
Seychelles, 132
Shaik, Shabir, 66
Shezi, Thandiwe, 27
*Shouting Silent* (documentary),
   121–122
Shumba, Precious, 136
Shuttleworth, Mark, 47
Sierra Leone, 120, 130, 131
Sikhala, Job, 105
Sirleaf, Ellen Johnson, 104
Sisulu, Walter, 16, 22
Sisulu, Zwelakhe, 16–17
Sithole, Xoliswa, 121–122
Smith, Charlene, 34, 63
soccer diplomacy, 105
social spending, 102
Somalia, 98, 136
Sorokobi, Yves, 130, 141
South Africa, 66, 74–81, 105,
   145n24
   and democracy, 7, 30, 61, 66,
      96, 112
   and economy, 45, 52–53
   Hunter-Gault's connection
      with, 2–3, 7, 111–115
   and journalism, 8, 112–113,
      115, 120–122, 126–127, 138
   and Kupe, 137–138
   and Libya, 95
   Medical Research Council of,
      31
   and music, 123

   National Assembly of, 62
   and NEPAD, 72, 97
   and peacekeeping, 99, 103
   and Rosebank, 7–12
   and Rwanda, 119
   and South African Council of
      Churches, 28
   transition of, 30, 60, 62, 115,
      127
   and TRC, 23–30, 26–28,
      113–114, 119, 126
   and Zimbabwe, 93, 133
   and Zuma, 67
   *See also* apartheid; HIV/AIDS;
      Mandela, Nelson
South African Broadcasting
   Corporation (SABC),
   126–127
sovereignty, 75, 79
Soviet Union, 4, 6
Soweto (township), 14–17, 36, 58
Sparks, Allister, 12, 24
Squires, Hillary, 66
Standard Bank, 52
Starr, Brenda, 142
Strand, Cynde, 41, 133
Stremlau, John, 100
students, 46. *See also* education
Sudan, 30, 98, 103–104, 104,
   120, 131
Sun City, 76
*Sunday Mail* (Zimbabwe news),
   133
*swaart gevaar*, 34, 64
Swaziland, 132